Josh McDowell's
FRIENDSHIP

WORKBOOK

Josh McDowell's
FRIENDSHIP

WORKBOOK

Dave Bellis
and
Ed Stewart

W PUBLISHING GROUP
A Division of Thomas Nelson Publishers
Since 1798

www.wpublishinggroup.com

JOSH MCDOWELL'S FRIENDSHIP 911 WORKBOOK

Unless otherwise indicated, Scripture quotations used in this book are from The New Living Translation, copyright © 1996. Used by permission of Tyndale House Publishers, Inc., Wheaton, Illinois 60189. All rights reserved.

Other Scripture references are from the following sources:

The Holy Bible, New International Version (NIV). Copyright © 1973, 1978, 1984, International Bible Society. Used by permission of Zondervan Bible Publishers.

New American Standard Bible (NASB), © 1960, 1977 by the Lockman Foundation.

All Scriptures quoted in dialogue are from the New Living Translation and the Holy Bible, New International Version.

Printed in the United States of America
00 01 02 03 04 05 QWD 9 8 7 6 5 4 3 2 1

CONTENTS

Acknowledgments

We want to acknowledge that the contents of the *Friendship 911 Workbook* have been drawn from a number of published works by Josh McDowell, especially the books from the PROJECT 911 Collection dealing with thoughts of suicide, past sexual abuse, death of a loved one, unplanned pregnancy, divorce of parents, finding true love, and conflicts with others. Josh McDowell's books *Disconnected Generation* and *Handbook on Counseling Youth* were also invaluable, as well as other PROJECT 911 resources.

We want to also acknowledge David Ferguson of Intimate Life Ministries for his influence on our lives personally and for sharing with us the principles that are represented in this workbook. David was instrumental in helping us mold and shape the content of the books in the PROJECT 911 Collection and therefore has made a significant contribution to this work as well.

We want to thank Bob Hostetler and Kevin Johnson for critiquing the workbook. Thanks to Becky Bellis for typing the workbook and providing insights into its development. And thanks to Jennifer Stair for her wise counsel and expert editing of the workbook.

—Dave Bellis
Ed Stewart

IMPORTANT:
Understand the Purpose of This Workbook

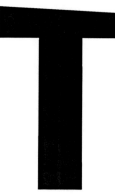here are study books and self-help books, comic books and cookbooks, fairy-tale books and true-to-life books. Some books make you feel good, others help you think new thoughts, and some provide practical instructions. But this book is different.

This workbook is designed to lead you to *experience* something. As you work through these exercises, you may think new ideas and even learn new things about yourself and others. But beyond that, you will experience the thrill of what is called **friendship**. You will discover what really makes friendship so valuable, why each of us so desperately needs friendship, and more importantly, how to experience friendship on a level you may have never thought possible. You will embark on a daily adventure to learn how to show true friendship and how to receive true friendship in return.

Wise Solomon said that "a friend is always loyal, and a brother [or sister] is born to help in time of need" (Prov. 17:17). You will discover throughout your workbook journey how to be a new kind of friend—a "911 friend." We call a 911 friend a trusted and loyal friend who will be there for us in time of real need, as Proverbs 17:17 says. You will also learn that if you become a 911 friend, someone will likely be there for you too.

This workbook is probably different than anything you have encountered before. It provides seven weeks of insights, with five Discovery Days for each week. Each day starts out with a dramatic story of students who are faced with some big challenges in which they need a certain kind of friend. Then through various fun and enlightening exercises, you will discover how you can be a 911 friend. Each Discovery Day should take about fifteen minutes of your time. The great thing about this workbook is that you won't be just learning what a true friend is; you will be experiencing true friendship!

How? You will be discovering what true friendship means by experiencing it with a "911 friendship partner." Select a friend of your same gender most likely from your youth group, who also is going through this workbook. On the fifth Discovery Day of each week, plan to get together with your friendship partner for at least a half-hour. Discovery Day Five gives instructions for how the two of you can experience the real truth about friendship.

The *Friendship 911 Workbook* is also designed to be used during weekly group meetings. In these group meetings, you will be able to discuss and share what you discovered through the lessons and how you and your partner have experienced deepened friendship. Your group meetings are really important in bonding your group together as committed friends.

You're about to begin a journey that could very well change your life forever. During the next seven weeks, you will experience the thrill of God involving you in *His* message and ministry of friendship. He will be teaching you what real relationships were meant to be— and that can be a life-changing experience!

WEEK ONE

A 911 Friend Is Available

SEAN'S STORY

he youth-group car wash raised $430 for scholarships to youth camp, but it will probably be better remembered for the riotous water fight. During a lull in the parade of dirty cars, the high-school seniors, led by energetic Sean Williams, commandeered the two hoses and opened fire on the rest of the group. The underclassmen fought back gamely with buckets and sponges filled with soapy water.

Caught in the crossfire during the battle were adult sponsors Doug and Jenny Shaw. But the Shaws, who claimed to be "thirty-something," had come prepared. As soon as the water started flying, Doug pulled an arsenal of high-powered water guns from the trunk of his car, and he and Jenny started spraying everyone. The good-natured, twenty-minute battle left the group drenched to the skin and sore from laughter. The good-natured soaking seemed to refresh the crew for the last two hours of work in the hot afternoon sun.

Sean was among the last to leave after cleanup, conveniently "forgetting" to ask for a ride home with some of his friends in the group. He had planned it that way. As Sean and Doug were stowing the last of the cleaning supplies in the church storage room, he asked, "Could I get a ride home with you and Jenny, if it's not too much trouble?"

Doug responded just as Sean had hoped. "Of course! It's no trouble at all." Sean smiled to himself. Doug and Jenny Shaw were very special people in his life. They had been there

for him when he really needed a friend. And he knew they would help him now with the burden he was carrying.

Doug suggested that they stop for burgers on the way home. Jenny and Sean wholeheartedly agreed, since they had been too busy washing cars—and spraying each other with water—to eat lunch.

"I need to talk to you two about something," Sean said soberly after they had placed their orders at the Burger Shack.

"I wondered if you had something on your mind," Jenny said. "You have been a little quieter than normal—except during today's water fight, of course."

Sean smiled briefly, then returned to his concern. "It's kind of serious, and I'm not sure what to do. So I'm hoping you have some suggestions."

Doug flashed an assuring smile. "We are more than happy to listen and to help if we can, Sean."

The waitress arrived with their drinks. Sean stirred his Coke gently with a straw as he composed his thoughts. "I'm worried about my friend Kev," he said at last.

"You mean Kevin Miller?" Jenny probed. "The guy who comes to church with you sometimes?"

"Kevin—right. A lot of us call him Kev. His parents are not Christians, but he says he has trusted Christ as his Savior. He's been acting strange lately."

"Is he in some kind of trouble?" Doug asked.

Sean released a long sigh. "I don't know for sure. He's been really quiet and distant for the last few weeks. And I have noticed a few other things that worry me."

Discovery Day

1

Doug leaned a little closer. "Like what?"

Sean felt odd talking about an issue that stirred up such painful memories. But he knew he had to confront it, for his friend's sake. "Well, things that make me wonder if Kev has had passing thoughts about suicide."

Jenny reached across the table and touched his arm. "This must be difficult for you, Sean. I'm sorry you have to deal with this issue again after what you have been through."

Sean felt a lump in his throat. He remembered all too clearly his bout with depression two years ago that pushed him to gulp down a fistful of sleeping pills. But Doug and Jenny were there at just the right moment. Sean would be forever grateful for the love and concern the Shaws had shown in his darkest hour.

"Thanks, I think I'm doing all right," he said, clearing his throat. "But I'm afraid for Kev. His parents are too busy fighting to pay much attention to him. His older brothers have moved away, so he's all alone at home. And when his friend Tim was killed in a car accident earlier this year, he really began to withdraw. I'm worried about him."

Doug spoke next. "What else is Kev doing that causes you to suspect he may have thought about suicide?"

"Some things that are painfully familiar. Kev seems tired all the time—he has zero energy. I call him at noon on Saturdays, and he's still in bed. Even when I talk him into coming over, he just wants to flop in a corner and go to sleep. He's been real moody too—angry one minute, silent the next."

"I'm so glad that you have been paying attention to Kevin's behavior, Sean," Jenny affirmed. "He seems to be crying out for help."

The waitress arrived with their burgers and fries. In his prayer of thanks for the food, Doug also prayed for Kevin Miller.

As they began to eat, Sean continued. "The thing that really bothers me is that Kev has been giving things away—even some great stuff, like his mountain bike. He doesn't

seem to care about anything. It's like he's not planning to stay around much longer."

Doug set his burger down after one bite. "Sean, do you know if Kev has ever attempted suicide before?"

"I don't think he has."

"Have you heard Kev actually say he wants to commit suicide?" Doug went on.

Sean shook his head. "I'm not with him all the time, of course. But he has never said anything like that to me."

"Have you seen any kind of a suicide note he may be working on?" Doug said.

"No, nothing like that."

Jenny asked, "Do you know what to do if he ever attempts suicide when you are around?"

Sean was silent for a moment. "I would do what you did for me," he said soberly. "I would get him to an emergency room right away. I would not leave him for a minute until he was in the care of a doctor."

The flashback was chillingly clear. One moment Sean was gulping down pills. The next moment—or so it seemed in his memory—he was in the emergency room with a tube down his throat. Doug and Jenny were there too, crying and praying. Sean's mother had called them in a panic when she discovered the empty bottle and could not wake her sleeping son. The youth sponsors had rushed Sean to the hospital and stayed with him until he was out of danger.

"And if Kev directly threatens suicide or if you find a suicide note," Jenny continued, "do you know what to do?"

Sean responded, "Call for help right away. Stay with him until he is in the care of a health professional."

"That's right," Jenny said. "I was sure you knew, but I wanted to hear you say it. Do you feel OK about taking such serious steps?"

"Absolutely," Sean said without hesitation. "Kev is my friend, and I don't want him to die. I'll do anything I can to help him. After all, someone cared enough to help me."

Your 911 Response

> **Alert!** If you ever hear someone talking about suicide, don't try to counsel him or her yourself. Get professional help immediately! Literally call 911 or contact a health professional. If you are unsure how to get the help your friend needs, contact your pastor, youth leader, or school counselor. Any talk of suicide must be taken seriously. It is important that you act immediately by getting professional help for your friend.

This Discovery Day is *not* about how to deal with suicidal people. It's about how to deal with friends who are experiencing certain feelings that sometimes lead to despair. People who think that suicide is their only option sometimes get there by means of a downward emotional spiral. Disappointment turns to discouragement, discouragement leads to depression, depression tumbles to despair, and despair prompts thoughts of suicide.

You may never hear someone talk about ending his or her life or know of anyone who has attempted suicide. But you do know people who experience disappointment, discouragement, and depression. These people need a 911 friend who "is always loyal . . . born to help in time of need" (Prov. 17:17). To be that kind of friend means you must be **available**.

Sean's friend Kev seems to be really hurting. Sean's worried about Kev, and that's a good start. As the story unfolds in the next few days, you will see how Sean's concern will lead him to play an important role in reversing the downward spiral of Kev's emotions. Sean's willingness to be available to Kev is the first step toward making him a 911 friend.

What Does It Mean to Be Available?

Put a check mark (✔) beside the phrases that convey to you the meaning of *being available*.

1. _____ Letting people work out their problems on their own.

2. _____ Saying, "Call me when things get better for you."

3. _____ Taking the time to listen to what someone has to say.

4. _____ Saying, "Here's a quarter; call someone who cares."

5. _____ Saying, "I'm going to be here for you, no matter what."

6. _____ Being available means we are interested enough in people to spend time listening to them and really caring about what happens in their world.

A Perfect Example of an Available Friend

> *"The LORD is close [available] to all who call on him"* (Ps. 145:18).

Jesus was a 911 friend to people, especially to hurting people. For example, a lot of people thought that Samaritans were real losers. But in John 4, Jesus made Himself available to the Samaritan woman at the well, and He talked with her about her life. The woman who was caught in adultery in John 8 was a nobody to everyone else, but Jesus was available to care for her too. Most people "freaked out" over lepers, but when ten lepers came to Jesus for healing in Luke 17, He was available to them.

Read Psalm 46:1.

What does this verse say God is to us? _____

God helps us in our _____

How does it make you feel to know that the God of the universe is available to you as a "safe place" (refuge) in time of trouble? Check (✔) all that apply.

- ❏ Disappointed
- ❏ Important
- ❏ Angry
- ❏ Hungry
- ❏ Humbled

- ❏ Grateful
- ❏ Afraid
- ❏ Secure
- ❏ Pleased
- ❏ _____

God will always be there for you, and He will never fail you. He wants you to be that kind of friend to others too.

Selecting Your Friendship Partner

Have you selected your 911 friendship partner with whom you are working through this workbook? If your youth leader has not helped you identify someone to go through this workbook with, find someone of your own gender this week to be your friendship partner.

This is *very important.* The fifth Discovery Day of each week calls for you to meet with your friendship partner. He or she will need a workbook too.

Check (✔) the box that applies.

❏ Yes, I have identified my 911 friendship partner, whose name is _____.

❏ No, I have not yet selected my 911 friendship partner, but I will do my best to do so within the next two days.

By going through this workbook with a friendship partner, you have the opportunity to move beyond learning about friendship to experiencing what true friendship is in your everyday life.

Prayer

Write a prayer, thanking God for being available to you and telling Him what that means to you. Then ask Him to help you be an available friend to your friendship partner this week.

Dear Lord, thank You for _____

_____

_____.

God, help me _____

_____

_____. Amen.

A **911** Friend Is Available

SEAN'S STORY CONTINUES

Sean smiled at Doug and Jenny. "I'm sure glad you two are willing to help me with Kev, because I don't want to wait until it's too late. So what can I do?"

"It's interesting that you would ask that, Sean," Doug began. "After your episode with the pills two years ago, Jenny and I realized that we did not know much about the warning signs for suicide. We were rather naive. We had heard the statistics: One thousand teenagers attempt suicide every day in our country, and eighteen of them actually succeed. But we didn't think that suicide was a problem Christian teens would face."

Jenny picked up the explanation. "Doug and I realize now that problems are problems, whether you're a Christian or not. Lots of kids suffer from stress, unfulfilled needs, and loneliness. Some live in families scarred by separation, divorce, and rejection. Some kids experience clinical depression. Others feel trapped in intolerable situations, looking for an easy way out. Many kids today are seriously starved for attention, and they will try anything to get it—even attempted suicide. Doug and I have learned to watch for the warning signs and to treat the cause, not just the symptom."

"That's what I want to do for Kev," Sean insisted. "Will you help me?"

"Of course," Doug assured.

By the time the trio finished their burgers, Sean had received several helpful tips for responding to Kevin's suspicious behavior. Doug concluded the chat by assuring Sean,

"We really admire your concern and commitment to help Kev. And we want you to know that we're here for you as you help him. Feel free to tell us how it's going and to call on us for help. We will be praying for you—and for Kev."

That night, Sean lay awake thinking about what Doug and Jenny had said. It was good advice, and he prayed that God would help him apply it in his friendship with Kev. And he prayed hard that Kev would not try anything foolish before he was able to show his friend how much he cared for him.

It seemed to take forever for Sean to find something Kev would do with him. They used to enjoy biking together, until Sean's friend shocked him by giving away an expensive mountain bike. Every other idea—playing video games, working out at the gym, going to the batting cages—was met with words like "I don't think so" or "I'm too tired."

But when Sean suggested that they speed skate the paved path along the river, Kev showed a spark of interest. So Sean arrived at Kev's house at 10:00 on a sunny Saturday morning to get him out of bed and help him find his roller blades and kneepads in the garage. By 11:30, they were gliding along the neighborhood sidewalks toward the river.

Kev didn't talk much as they cruised along the tree-lined path. Sean, who was a better skater, let his friend lead. Following Kev, Sean prayed that God would increase his compassion for his friend and give him words that would help Kev talk about his disturbing behavior.

Reaching the halfway point, Kev was out of breath. So Sean suggested that they take a

Discovery Day

2

breather near the path. Kev quickly agreed. They flipped off their kneepads and collapsed on a bench facing the river.

"This is really cool, Kev," Sean said, passing a water bottle to his friend. "We haven't done anything like this in a long time."

"Yeah, I know," Kev said, breathing hard. He took a swallow and stared out at the river. Sean noted his friend's appearance. He wore faded black shorts and a ragged black T-shirt emblazoned with the image of a rock group posed in a cemetery. His sad-looking face was framed by stringy hair. Kev used to be more conscientious about his appearance, even when doing something athletic. Sean felt sad because his friend didn't seem to care about himself anymore.

Encouraged from his talk with Doug and Jenny, Sean decided to break the ice. "Kev, I've been wanting to talk to you about something," he began cautiously.

Kev continued to gaze out at the river, saying nothing.

Sean continued. "We haven't been doing as much stuff together lately. Is everything all right . . . I mean, with us?"

Kev shrugged. "Yeah, everything is OK, I guess."

"It just seems like you haven't wanted to do much lately."

"I've been kind of busy."

Sean paused, hoping he didn't sound too nosy. Then he said, "You've seemed a little down lately. Is everything else OK?"

Kev didn't answer for several moments. Then he finally looked at Sean. "Not exactly," he said at last, a shadow of pain drifting past his face.

"Is it something I can help with?" Sean probed.

Kev looked away again, then he dropped his head and stared at the ground. Finally he said, "Not unless you can keep my parents from getting a divorce or turn all my Fs into Cs at school."

Your 911 Response

Kev was clearly depressed, so it was pretty easy for Sean to recognize his friend's need for 911 care. But what about your friends? Perhaps none of them is seriously depressed like Kev. How can you know when you really need to be available to your friends? There are at least three telltale signs you need to watch for:

1. **Disappointment.** People become disappointed when their hopes or expectations are not met. Most disappointments are relatively minor, but they still hurt.
2. **Discouragement.** When disappointments pile up, they can lead to discouragement. When people are discouraged, their hope and confidence grow weak, and they begin to lose heart.
3. **Depression.** When people are discouraged for a long period of time, they may experience long periods of low spirits, gloominess, dejection, sadness, and withdrawal from others.

Some of your friends might be experiencing disappointment, discouragement, and depression, but you may not even know it. Many students do a good job of hiding their true feelings. The more you become known as a caring person who is willing to make yourself available to others, the more your friends will open up and share their feelings.

Being an available friend includes learning how to tell when someone is disappointed, discouraged, or depressed. You can always ask someone, "How are you doing—really?" but it is also helpful to know what disappointment, discouragement, and depression look like and sound like.

A World Where Disappointment, Discouragement, or Depression Exists

Look over the following situations and check (✔) any that someone you know may have experienced during the last several months.

- ❑ Unresolved conflict with someone
- ❑ Recent criticism from an influential person
- ❑ Physical separation from a loved one
- ❑ Desire for a relationship that hasn't happened
- ❑ Physical illness or accident
- ❑ Recent breakup of a relationship
- ❑ Recent death of a loved one

- ❑ Cut from a team
- ❑ Recent separation/divorce of parents
- ❑ Loss of a big game or competition
- ❑ Failing grade at school
- ❑ Financial pressure
- ❑ Loss of an important job

If any of your friends has experienced one or more of the above situations, you may hear them say something that communicates that they are:

- ✳ feeling misunderstood
- ✳ feeling unimportant
- ✳ feeling rejected
- ✳ feeling lonely
- ✳ feeling misrepresented

- ✳ feeling unloved
- ✳ feeling unneeded
- ✳ feeling like a failure
- ✳ feeling like they don't belong
- ✳ feeling unproductive

Have you heard your friendship partner or someone else express any of these feelings? If so, briefly describe the situation, including how he or she may have experienced some of these feelings. If your friendship partner has not experienced such a situation, describe one that someone else has experienced.

_____ (friend's name) has recently experienced _____

_____

_____

He or she has expressed feelings like:_____

_____

_____

God Wants Your Friends to Know That He Is Available to Them

God wants your friends to tell Him about their worries and cares and troubles.

Read 1 Peter 5:7.

Based on this verse, what does God want us to do with our worries and cares?

_____

Why?_____

Because God cares for us when we are disappointed, discouraged, and depressed, He wants us to come to Him. He promises to help us with our troubles.

"So let us come boldly to the throne of our gracious God. There we will receive his mercy, and we will find grace to help us when we need it" (Heb. 4:16).

God Wants Your Friends to Know That You Are Available to Them

God also wants to involve you as a 911 friend who will give of yourself to help others. The apostle Paul instructs us:

"Live a life filled with love for others, following the example of Christ, who loved you and gave himself as a sacrifice to take away your sins" (Eph. 5:2).

You may have understood that Christ loved you and gave of Himself for you, but did you know you are supposed to love others and give of yourself too?

❑ Yes   ❑ No   ❑ Wasn't Sure

You may wonder if being available to share in someone else's problems and troubles will just drain you. It shouldn't. Becoming a 911 friend is actually very exciting and fulfilling, because God is involving you in *His* ministry of caring in the life of your friend. God is the source for meeting your friend's need (see Ps. 46:1), and He wants you to join Him in being an available "help in time of need" (Prov.17:17).

Prayer

Write a prayer telling God that you are available to minister His care and love this week to your friends, especially to your friendship partner.

Dear Father, I offer myself _____

_____

_____

_____

_____

_____

_____

And help me to know how to be more available this week to:

_____ (friendship partner's name).

_____ (another friend's name).

Amen.

A 911 Friend Is Available

SEAN'S STORY CONTINUES

Your parents are getting a divorce?" Sean said with surprise.

Kevin nodded slowly. "Mom found out Dad has a 'girlfriend' at the office. So she kicked him out and told him she didn't even want him to see me. It's been awful at our house."

Sean touched his friend's shoulder. "Man, Kev, I'm sorry. I knew your mom and dad were having trouble. But divorce . . . that's tough."

Head drooping low, Kev blinked hard a couple of times and rubbed his nose. Sean had never seen his friend look so sad. He felt a lump of sorrow for him swelling in his throat.

"If you want to talk about it," Sean went on, "I mean, how you feel and all, I'm here."

Kev glanced at him almost scornfully. "You don't need to do that, Sean."

"Do what?"

"I mean you don't have to get involved. You have your own problems to deal with. You don't want to hear about mine."

"Kev, we're friends, and I—"

"So we go biking and skating sometimes," Kev interrupted. "That doesn't mean you have to take on my problems."

"Hey, we're friends, remember?" Sean insisted. "If you're bummed out and there is something I can do to help, I'm available—even if it just means listening to you."

Kev looked back toward the river, thinking. Sean prayed silently for his friend.

"It may be too late to help me," Kev said, just above a whisper.

The words sent a chill down Sean's spine. "What do you mean?"

"I mean, what's the point? My parents hate each other, and they can't stand me. My brothers think I'm a pest. I'm messing up in all my classes. My best friend, Tim, was killed, and my friends don't want to hang out with me—except for you."

"You really miss Tim, don't you?" Sean said. "I'm sad you feel so alone. And I didn't realize school was so hard for you right now. I'm sorry, Kev."

Kev released a sharp sigh. Sean could see the pain in his face. "I'm just a waste of space on this planet, and I'm so tired of being in the way."

Sean jabbed his elbow at his friend. "You are *not* a waste of space," he said. "You're a really cool guy. Whenever you feel like a waste of space, you just call me, and I'll talk some sense into you. Remember, God loves you, and I think you're OK too—except you're a lousy skater."

Kev chuckled under his breath as he lightly punched Sean's shoulder. "Thanks, man," he said.

After a few moments of silence, Kev began describing how bad he felt about his parents splitting up about the same time his friend died. He said he had a stomachache almost all the time and that he just wanted to sleep. Unable to concentrate, his grades had suffered terribly. Kev didn't think that he would ever catch up in school, nor did he feel it was worth trying.

"I'm really bummed for you, Kev," Sean said, looking straight ahead "It hurts me that you have to go through all this stuff."

Kev also spoke about feeling rejected by his brothers and feeling lonely without his friends. "I know it's tough," Sean assured him. "But I'm your friend, and I know we'll get through all this, OK?" Then Sean prayed a simple prayer for Kev just loud enough for God and his friend to hear.

Your 911 Response

It's great that Kev has a 911 friend like Sean at this difficult time in his life. Maybe you can identify with how Kev feels to have a friend be there for you when you were disappointed, discouraged, or depressed. Can you think of a friend who was available to you at a difficult time in your life? If so, describe the situation by completing any of the following statements that apply:

The friend who was available to me was _____(friend's name).

I was disappointed, and my friend _____

_____

_____

_____

I was discouraged, and my friend _____

_____

_____

_____

I was depressed, and my friend _____

_____

_____

_____

Having an available friend made me feel _____

_____

_____

_____

If you've ever had a 911 friend like Sean, you remember feeling cared for and important to someone. That feeling doesn't come so much from what friends *do* but from who they *are*—true friends. Friendship is not so much about *doing* things as it is about *being* a friend. Doing for your friends is important, but doing must come from who you are as a true friend.

Here are three vital qualities for being an available 911 friend: (1) be interested, (2) be a listener, and (3) be a safe zone.

Be Interested

Being interested means really caring about your friend and about what he or she is going through. It means caring enough to invest your time and to get involved in your friend's world.

What does being interested look like and sound like? Check (✔) the actions below that may demonstrate your sincere interest in a friend:

❑ Waiting to return your friend's call until he or she gets over whatever.

❑ Scheduling time to spend with your friend at a time convenient to him or her.

❑ Saying, "I'm here for you, and with God's help we'll get through this together."

❑ Sending your friend a bouquet of plastic flowers with a note that reads, "Get on with your life."

❑ Saying, "I'll be calling you to see how you're doing."

❑ Taking your friend's need to God in prayer.

Be a Listener

Listening is more than just cleaning the wax out of your ears. Listening is one way you come to understand and identify with what your friend is feeling. If you don't really listen, the time you spend with a friend in need doesn't mean much. Check (✔) the actions below that might reflect being a good listener to a friend:

❑ Turning toward your friend, maintaining eye contact, and nodding in response as he or she speaks.

❑ Keeping your CD earphones on but turning the volume down from 9 to 6.

❑ Occasionally asking something like, "What do you mean by that?" or "Why is that important to you?"

❑ Looking at your watch often so your friend knows your time is important to you.

❑ Refraining from interrupting your friend or finishing his or her sentences.

❑ Demanding that your friend listen to you as long as you had to listen to him or her.

Be a Safe Zone

Psalm 46:1 says, "God is our refuge." A refuge is a safe place. Being a 911 friend requires being a safe place for your friend. Your friend needs to feel that the struggles he or she shares with you won't be broadcast all over school and the community. Being a safe zone means you treat information with confidentiality, allowing your friend to feel safe about sharing his or her struggles. Check (✔) the actions below that suggest you are a safe zone for your friend:

❑ Secretly recording your friend's comments to play at your next party.

❑ Making sure you talk to your friend privately where others cannot accidentally overhear.

❑ Saying, "I won't share what you tell me with anyone unless you want me to"—and meaning it.

❑ Only sharing what was told you in confidence with twenty or thirty others who promise not to tell anyone else.

❑ Submitting a detailed article about your friend's problems to the school newspaper but changing his or her name slightly.

❑ Refusing to share what was told you in confidence with others, even if you leave out your friend's name.

Being an **available** friend means that you are *interested* in your friend's struggles, that you *listen* attentively and identify with what your friend is going through, and that you are a *safe zone* so your friend is comfortable sharing his or her struggles with you

Are you this kind of available friend? Is someone an available friend to you? How do you and your friends rate as available friends? Circle the number on each scale that reflects how you rate yourself and your friends.

The Interested Scale

1	2	3	4	5	6	7	8	9	10
not very interested				somewhat interested				very interested	

I would rate myself a _____ for being interested in my friends' problems and struggles.

I would rate my friends a _____ for being interested in my problems and struggles.

The Listening Scale

1	2	3	4	5	6	7	8	9	10
not a very good listener				a somewhat good listener				a very good listener	

I would rate myself a _____ for listening to my friends' problems and struggles.

I would rate my friends a _____ for listening to my problems and struggles.

The Safe Zone Scale

1	2	3	4	5	6	7	8	9	10
not very safe				somewhat safe				very safe	

I would rate myself a _____ for being a safe zone in keeping conversations confidential.

I would rate my friends a _____ for being a safe zone in keeping conversations confidential.

Are you satisfied with your ratings as an available 911 friend? Do you have one or more friends who rank high as available friends? Everyone has room for improvement. Learning to become a more available friend is a process that takes effort and practice.

Schedule the Meeting Time with Your Friendship Partner

Call your friendship partner and schedule a time and place to get together in two days to work through Discovery Day Five together. If you haven't selected a friendship partner yet, it's still not too late to do so.

A Prayer for You

Read the following prayer. This is the prayer your youth leader has been encouraged to pray for you. The writers of this workbook have prayed this for you too.

Dear Father,

   Thank You for being the perfect available friend to us. You are always there caring for us, listening to us, and You are the safest place ever. Let _____ (your name) know in a special way today that You are a loyal friend who will never fail. Give him/her courage and strength to share with his or her friendship partner how he/she wants to become a better friend—a friend like You. Thank You again for being You, and thank You for Your Son, who is our best friend. Thank you that He reassures us with His words, "And be sure of this: I am with you always, even to the end of the age" (Matt. 28:20).

In Jesus' name, amen.

Discovery Day 4

L et's speed skate to the end of the path and eat," Sean said. Skating behind Kev again, Sean thanked God silently for the opportunity to be there for his friend. He knew that their brief chat on the riverside bench was only a beginning. Sean was eager to continue with the suggestions Doug and Jenny had provided.

When they reached the end of the path, Sean unloaded his backpack and took out the sandwiches he had packed. The two pulled off their skates and socks and dipped their feet in the river as they ate sandwiches and tortilla chips. The gentle breeze off the river felt refreshing. Sean noticed that Kev's face was a little brighter, and he knew it was more than the sunshine.

"So, what's up with you at school?" Sean mumbled through a mouthful of chips. "Which classes are giving you the most trouble? How far behind are you?"

Kev groaned at the reminder of his failing grades. "I guess you can't keep it from friends, can you?" he said wryly.

"I'm not trying to make you feel bad," Sean interjected quickly. "I just thought maybe I can help."

"There's only a month left in the semester, Sean," he said. "Even Einstein couldn't dig me out of this hole." He went on to explain that he was failing in biology and American lit, and he was barely passing in three other classes. He had missed a number of homework assignments, which left him unprepared for several exams he had either failed or nearly failed.

Sean listened intently. Then he said, "Maybe we can't pull all your grades up to As or Bs. But I'll bet we can pull most of them up to Cs. At least you'll pass. How does that sound?"

"You want to help me get my grades up?" Kev said with a look of disbelief. "Why? Do you like schoolwork that much?"

Sean smiled. "You know better than that. It's just that I want to help, that's all. That's what friends are for. I know some other kids at church who would be willing to help too."

"You mean, you guys would be willing to cheat for me?"

"I'm not talking about doing your work for you," Sean explained. "I'm talking about helping you sort through your missing assignments to get you caught up, studying together for tests, and things like that."

"Kind of like tutoring," Kev put in.

"Right. I do pretty well in the lit and history areas, so I can help you there. Rachel DeWitt is a science whiz, so she could probably help you catch up in biology. What do you think?"

"Rachel's cool. I like her," Kev responded.

The two were silent for several moments. "I don't know what to think," Kev began. "Nobody's offered to help me like this, not even my parents—at least, not since Tim died. I pretty much felt like I was in it alone—you know, sink or swim. It was getting harder and harder to stay afloat in school and at home."

"Well, it's not like that anymore, Kev," Sean assured. "I'm sorry it took so long to realize how tough things were getting for you. But I want to help. I know others in the youth group do too, including Doug and Jenny—if that's OK with you."

"Yeah," he said at last, "that's OK. Thanks."

Kev seemed happier during the skate back home. Sean also noticed a burst of energy in his friend that at times made it difficult for him to keep up. It was good to see Kev getting back to his old, energetic self.

That night Sean decided he would call Kev or spend time with him at school each day, just to touch base and show his interest. And whenever the weather cooperated, Sean intended to get Kev out speed skating on the riverside path.

Your 911 Response

Sean is really learning to be an available 911 friend, isn't he? He is tapping into an important secret that you also need to discover if you want to become a true 911 friend. Here's the secret: **You must sincerely believe that you don't know how to be a 911 friend!** Seriously, the secret to being an available 911 friend—a friend who is interested, who listens, and who is a safe zone for others—is to admit that you can't be that kind of friend—on your own, that is. Even though you may not want to admit it, you don't have what it really takes to be a 911 friend. Nobody does.

"Apart from me you can do nothing" (John 15:5).

"For my thoughts are not your thoughts, neither are your ways, my ways" (Isa. 55:8 NIV)

Be honest! Do you feel that you have in yourself all the strength and wisdom you need to be a 911 friend?

❑ **Yes**   ❑ **Maybe I do a little**   ❑ **No**

We sometimes tend to answer "yes" or "maybe I do a little." If you answered that way, why do you tend to think you have the strength and wisdom in yourself to be an available friend?

_____

_____

_____

Unlocking Your Power Source

"OK," you respond. "I'll drop the 'I've-got-it-all-together' attitude and accept that I don't have the power in myself to be a 911 friend. So what does it take to be a consistent 911 friend?"

Being a consistent 911 friend means you must admit to God that you need His help and then depend on Christ for the power and strength to be the kind of 911 friend that He is. Admitting that you are weak and in need of help may be humbling, but depending on Christ's strength is empowering!

The apostle Paul understood the secret of humbly admitting his own weakness and being empowered with Christ's strength. He said:

"For [Christ] has said to me, 'My grace is sufficient for you, for power is perfected in weakness.' Most gladly, therefore, I will boast about my weaknesses, that the power of Christ may dwell in me" (2 Cor. 12:9 NASB).

Will you admit that *you* don't have the power to always be a caring and interested friend to people who are struggling? Will you depend on Christ to be more caring like He is?

❑ **Yes**   ❑ **I'll try**

Will you admit that *you* don't have the strength to always be a good listener to others in need? Will you depend upon Christ to be a better listener like He is?

❑ **Yes**   ❑ **I'll try**

Will you admit that *you* don't have the resources to always be a trusted safe zone, keeping your friends' comments and feelings confidential? Will you depend on Christ to be a better safe zone like He is?

❑ **Yes**   ❑ **I'll try**

Say this verse out loud to God:

"For I can do everything with the help of Christ who gives me the strength I need" (Phil. 4:13).

You *can* be more Christlike and a better friend to others with His help and His strength! He will help you to admit your weakness and to depend more upon His strength.

But how do we tap into God's strength to become a better Christlike 911 friend? Check (✔) the box that seems most correct.

❑ Chant Philippians 4:13 three times each day
❑ Date a superspiritual person
❑ Listen to Christian rock music
❑ Memorize every verse in the Old and New Testament so you can quote it backward.

❑ Leave school and live in solitude with monks
❑ Allow God to continually live and love through you by the power of His Spirit

Read the following verses thoughtfully:

"Dear friends, let us continue to love one another, for love comes from God . . . If we love each other, God lives in us, and his love has been brought to full expression through us. And God has given us his Spirit as proof that we live in him and he in us . . . God is love, and all who live in love live in God, and God lives in them. And as we live in God, our love grows more perfect" (1 John 4:7–17).

Your power source for being a more Christlike 911 friend is the Holy Spirit of God living and working inside you. As a Christian, you are God's child, and His Spirit of love lives inside you. But you must allow His love to grow in you every day. Being a Christlike 911 friend is a growing process "as we live in God."

Throughout the *Friendship 911 Workbook*, you will discover how to actually "live in God" and experience God's love working through you to be a true friend. As you depend on God and act in obedience to His Word, He will empower you to be a more caring friend, a better listener, a safer place, and much more. And you will also find that God may very well empower your friends to be 911 friends to you.

Prayerful Meditation

Take a few moments to think of your friendship partner. At times, your friend needs someone to really care, to listen, and to be a safe zone for talking through struggles. Now imagine Christ personally being that 911 friend to your friendship partner.

Sense Christ's compassionate heart as He walks up to your friend and says, "I really care what is happening to you right now. I know what it's like to hurt like you hurt, and it hurts Me that you hurt. I want you to know that I'm here for you, no matter what."

As you stand there watching Christ share this with your friend, can you sense His caring heart? Tell Christ right now that you want His compassionate heart to touch your own heart.

_____

_____

_____

Imagine now that you, your friend, and Christ are sitting alone in a quiet place. Your friend begins to open up and share with Jesus the details of his or her struggle and how it makes him or her feel. You see Jesus lean forward, taking in every word. You see the pain reflected in His face as he nods His head slowly in understanding. You hear Him say in a soft voice, "I'm really sorry you're going through all this." You look closer and see tears of compassion filling the Savior's eyes and spilling down His cheek. Can you feel Christ's understanding and how He identifies with your friend's struggles? Why don't you tell Jesus how you want His understanding heart to be yours?

_____

_____

_____

Finally, your friend shared with Jesus all he or she is going to share. But just as your friend is about to get up, Christ reaches out and touches his or her arm. In a tender voice, He says, "I want you to know that what we've talked about here will stay here. You never have to worry that I will tell your problem to someone else. I'm your safe place. You can always come to me without fear of rejection or ridicule. I'll be your refuge now and forever. You can count on it. I'll always, *always* be your truest friend."

Can you see the loyalty in Christ's gaze? Can you hear it in His voice? Tell Christ right now that you want His loyalty to be yours too.

_____

_____

_____

Confirm Your Meeting Time with Your Friendship Partner

Call your friendship partner today and confirm your scheduled time to go over Discovery Day Five together: _____ (date); _____ (time); _____ (place).

A *911* Friend Is Available

SEAN'S STORY CONTINUES

Discovery Day 5

Sean and Kev walked the seven blocks from the high school to Doug Shaw's house. Sean noted with secret delight that Kev looked and sounded much better than he had two weeks ago during their skate and chat. Sean had said nothing to his friend about his appearance, but Kev's colorful clothes and combed hair told him that his friend was feeling much better about himself.

Only a few days after their Saturday power skate together, Kev admitted what Sean had suspected. "You'll probably think I'm some kind of psycho," he had said one day as they watched a school volleyball match, "but I was beginning to wonder if my life was worth living. Compared to how bad things were, dying didn't seem too bad."

Sean assured Kev that he was no "psycho." A few days later, Sean asked if Kev would like to meet with Doug Shaw, the youth-group sponsor, to talk about his problems at home. Kev agreed—if Sean would go with him. Sean promised to do so. The meeting had been set for today after school.

Doug turned into the driveway as Sean and Kev approached the house. The youth sponsor, who operated a small quick-print shop in town, had taken off work early to meet Sean and Kev. Once inside, Doug grabbed three sodas out of the fridge, and they sat down to enjoy their drinks.

In response to Doug's nonthreatening questions, Kev talked about his parents' impending divorce, his loneliness, and his problems at school, mentioning that he had briefly thought of ending his life. Sean was proud of his friend for being so honest, even though he could see it was hard for Kev to talk about these painful issues.

"I would like to make a simple contract with you, Kev," Doug said with an assuring smile. "You are very important to Sean and me and to others in our youth group. I would like you to agree to call me immediately whenever the idea of suicide even crosses your mind. And I agree to respond immediately when you call and take time to talk with you. Will you make this contract with me?" Doug held out his hand for a handshake of agreement.

Sean glanced at Kev, unsure how he would respond to Doug's offer. Finally Kev said, "OK. I don't think I will ever think seriously about suicide again, but I promise to call you if I do. Thanks." Then he gripped Doug's hand and shook it. Doug promised to pray for Kev every day for the next few weeks.

Doug placed his Bible on the table. "I thought we could have a short Bible study on the topic of how God sees us. When we see ourselves as God sees us, we begin to realize how important we are to Him and to others." Sean and Kev reached into their backpacks and pulled out the small Bibles they carried to school.

Doug instructed them to turn to Jeremiah 31:3. The boys flipped pages until they reached the passage. "Sean, why don't you read that verse aloud for us?" Doug asked.

Sean cleared his throat and read, "'The LORD appeared to us in the past, saying: "I have loved you with an everlasting love; I have drawn you with loving-kindness."'"

Doug asked, "According to this verse, how does God see us?"

Sean purposely held back to allow Kev a chance to answer. "He loves us, so I guess He sees us as lovable," Kev responded.

"That's right," Doug said. "God sees you as lovable. He loves you with an everlasting love. He loves you no matter what you have done, no matter how miserable your life is, no matter how big your problems are, no matter how many mistakes you have made or sins you have committed. God never stops loving you . . . and He never will."

Doug referred to a few more verses that emphasized God's abiding love. Kev seemed most impressed by Isaiah 49:16: "I have engraved you on the palms of my hands." He remarked, "Wow, God loves us so much that He has tattooed our names on His hands! That's cool." Sean and Doug smiled at Kev's enthusiasm.

Next, Doug directed them to Genesis 1:27, Romans 8:3–5, 1 Peter 1:18–19, and Ephesians 2:10. Kev answered the question before Doug could ask it. "God also sees us as very valuable. He created us in His image, just a little lower than the angels. He gave up His own Son to die on the cross for our sins. He calls us His work of art, His masterpiece. And He has a plan to bless us and prosper us. That means we are very special to God."

The next set of verses focused on the Holy Spirit, concluding with Philippians 4:13, which Kev read: "I can do everything with the help of Christ who gives me the strength I need." Sean answered Doug's question this time. "These verses say that God sees us as very useful to Him. He has given us gifts and abilities, He has sent His Holy Spirit to live in us, and He calls us to serve Him with the strength He provides."

Doug nodded enthusiastically. "We are not perfect, and sometimes we feel very helpless. But God gives us His Holy Spirit to live in us and be our Helper. Second Corinthians 5:19 says that He has entrusted us with the ministry of reaching others for him. Isn't it amazing that God trusts imperfect people like us to bring others to Him!"

"I never thought about it that way," Kev put in, eyebrows arched in surprise.

Doug focused on Kev. "How does it make you feel, knowing that our perfect, all-powerful God sees you as lovable, valuable, and useful?"

Kev considered the question for several seconds. Then he said, "Part of me feels like God hasn't taken a very close look at me, because I don't see myself that way. But another part of me feels kind of honored that He does see me that way."

Sean posed the next question for Kev. "Who do you think sees you for who you really are: you or God?"

Kev thought about it, then he flashed an impish smile. "That's a trick question. Who would claim that they see things better than God does?"

Doug and Sean chuckled at Kev's response. Then Doug said, "That's just the point, Kev. God doesn't make mistakes, and He doesn't have a vision problem. If He sees you as lovable, valuable, and useful—and the Bible says that He does—then that's what you are. Right?"

Kev smiled and shrugged. "Right."

Doug continued, talking, "I believe that God wants us to see ourselves as He sees us. That's how we gain the confidence to deal with the hard things in our lives. We can get through anything if we know that God loves us, values us, and desires to use us."

Kev was suddenly sober. "Even the breakup of a family? Even the horrible death of a close friend?"

Doug reached out and touched his arm. "What do you think, Kev?" he responded.

Kev studied the understanding faces of his friend and youth leader. "Yeah," he said at last, "I think God can help me get through these things, because I guess I'm sorta lovable, valuable, and useful to Him. I guess that running away from my problems was a bad idea, if God thinks I'm OK."

"I think you're exactly right, Kev," Doug responded, smiling. "God thinks you're OK, and so do we."

Your 911 Response

The turnaround taking place in Kev's life began when Sean made himself available to Kev and shared God's love by being interested, being a listener, and being a safe zone—an available friend. But as we've said before, everyone needs an available friend, not just people with "big" problems. People like you and your friendship partner need an available friend too.

A Friendship Partner Exercise

Walk through the following exercise with your friendship partner. Take turns responding to each other as you answer each question or statement.

It is ☐ Easy   ☐ Somewhat hard   ☐ Quite hard to admit that I need someone to be an available friend to me (someone who's interested, listens, and is a safe zone for me).

In the lines below, write down why you answered the way you did and tell it to your friend. [NOTE: Some guys, as well as girls, find sharing their true feelings harder to do than others. It may take some getting used to, but it will be worth it.]

_____

_____

_____

_____

_____

How did it feel to admit to your friendship partner that you needed an available friend?

_____

_____

_____

_____

_____

Remember how you scored yourself on the "interested," "listening," and "safe zone" scales? Regardless of how you scored yourself, express to your friendship partner that you want to be a friend who shows a greater interest, who listens better, and who is a safer place for him or her.

On the lines below, record how your friend responds to your desire to be a better friend to him or her.

_____

_____

_____

_____

_____

_____

Take some time to listen to what your friendship partner has to say about anything that was particularly meaningful or interesting to him or her from the first four Discovery Days. Take turns listening to what each other has to say. Record your insights here.

_____

_____

_____

_____

_____

_____

Commit to meeting together each week to walk through Discovery Day Five of each week. Be prepared to share this week's interaction with each other at your group meeting.

Close your time by writing out a prayer, asking the Holy Spirit to live and love through you during these next few weeks as you discover how to experience Christlike 911 friendship.

_____

_____

_____

_____

_____ Amen.

The PROJECT 911 Collection

The story of Sean and Kevin in this workbook is adapted from the small book entitled *My Friend Is Struggling with Thoughts of Suicide*. The book is designed as a giveaway book that you can read and then give to a friend whom you sense may be struggling with thoughts of suicide. Beyond the fictional story, this book provides insights and helpful instruction for your friend. As noted in the very first Discovery Day, if someone you know shows signs of actually attempting suicide, get immediate help by literally calling 911. Don't just give them a book!

But if you know someone who has seemed depressed for a period of time, this book may be of great help.

If you want one or more of these books for a friend, contact your youth leader. He or she may have some copies on hand. If not, this and other books in this collection may be ordered in bulk by calling 1-800-933-9673 ext. 9-2039. Or you may purchase copies of this book at your local Christian bookstore.

WEEK TWO

ANN'S STORY

The little girl stiffened with fear as she heard soft footsteps coming down the hall. Alone in her grandparents' darkened guest bedroom, she thought about slipping out of the bed and hiding underneath it. But hearing the doorknob slowly turn, she knew it was too late. So she pulled the covers over her head and crawled to the bottom of the bed, hoping somehow he wouldn't find her.

She heard him step into the room. "Pumpkin, it's me, Grandpa," she heard him whisper. "Grandma is sound asleep, so we can have our secret visit now." The little girl squeezed herself into a tight ball at the bottom of the bed, wishing she could make herself smaller, wishing she could even disappear. She didn't like Grandpa's "secret visits." He touched her where she didn't like being touched. But she couldn't tell anyone about the touching because Grandpa said it was a secret. Besides, she didn't want to tell anyone because she thought she would get in trouble for doing such a bad thing.

The little girl heard the bedroom door close. "Come on out, sweetie," Grandpa whispered. She cringed as her grandfather's hands patted the covers until he found the lump at the bottom.

"No secret visit, Grandpa," she said as he began slowly peeling away the covers. "Please, Grandpa, no—no—no!"

"Wake up, wake up!" Ann felt someone jostling her gently by the shoulder. "You're having a nightmare, Annie. Wake up." The whispering voice she heard was not her grandfather's. It sounded like Heather's voice.

After another jostle, Ann snapped fully awake with a start. Heather was shaking her, and it was dark. Ann suddenly remembered she was in a sleeping bag in her bunk at summer church camp. Heather and four other girls from church were in the cabin with her. Their adult counselor, Jenny Shaw, was there too.

Ann released a sigh of relief. She was not six years old as she had been in her terrible dream; she was fourteen now. And she was not with her grandfather; she was with her friends at camp. Yet the dream had left her heart beating rapidly, and she was drenched with sweat even in the cool, rustic mountain cabin.

"Ann, are you all right?" Heather whispered. "You were saying, 'No, Grandpa, no.' It sounded like you were in pain."

Ann could barely make out her friend's face in the darkness. "Yeah, I'm all right," she said, just above a whisper. "Like you said, it was just a bad dream. I'm fine now."

Heather continued in a hushed tone. "It sounded awful, like your grandfather was chasing you with an ax or something."

"I'm sorry I woke you up," Ann said, diverting attention from the dream. "I hope I didn't wake up the whole cabin."

"Don't worry," Heather assured her, "everybody else is still sawing logs."

Ann Cassidy considered Heather Wells the best of all possible friends. Heather had been like a sister—always there for her, always concerned. Their friendship had begun in the fifth grade when Ann's mother enrolled her in Faith Christian School. Ann thought it was odd when Mom put her in a Christian school, especially since her family did not attend church. But it worked out for the best.

In that first year at Faith, Ann met two people who became very special to her. First, she met Heather Wells in Mr. Trotter's fifth-grade class. Second, she met Jesus Christ through the worship and Bible teaching in the weekly chapel service. Ann trusted Christ in October of that first year and began attending church with Heather on Sundays. They had been like sisters ever since.

"So what were you dreaming about?" Heather pressed with sisterly nosiness.

Ann didn't want to answer. She had had the same dream many times before. It always left her feeling dirty and empty, because she knew it was more than a bad dream. It was also a bad memory.

"It was nothing, really," Ann said, aware that she was not telling the whole truth. "We should go back to sleep."

"Are you having problems with your grandfather, Annie?" Heather pried, still whispering. "Is it something you want me to pray about?"

One of the many things Ann appreciated about Heather was that she prayed about everything. "Grandpa Bennett died two years ago," Ann answered.

"Oh, sorry. I just thought. . . . " Heather's voice trailed off.

"No problem," Ann said. "Let's get back to sleep. Are we still having morning devotions together?"

"Of course. Out by the archery range right after breakfast."

"OK, good night," Ann whispered. "And thanks."

"Good night."

Ann was still awake when she heard deep, noisy breaths coming from the bunk next to hers. Heather was asleep. *I didn't exactly tell you the truth, Heather,* Ann confessed silently. *I don't have any problems with Grandpa now, because he's dead. I have never told anyone about what Grandpa did to me. He said it was our secret. Now I'm so ashamed about what happened that I'm afraid to tell anyone. And I can't seem to get these awful memories to go away. Maybe it is something I need you to pray with me about.*

Your 911 Response

You don't have to be a genius to figure out what has happened to Ann. It's called sexual abuse, and the experience and its memories are causing Ann a lot of pain. Why hasn't she told anyone about her grandpa's "secret visits" before? Why has she suffered in silence for so long? Like a lot of people in similar situations, Ann is afraid of what people will think about her. She is ashamed of what happened to her, even though it wasn't her fault. Ann suffers in part from false guilt, and she's afraid that people won't accept her for who she is. She is suffering from a sense of low self-worth.

You may or may not know anyone who has gone through the terrifying experience of childhood sexual abuse. But you can be sure there are students all around you who, like Ann, suffer from a sense of low self-worth. Many people today feel they are unloved, unlovable, and unworthy of acceptance. They need to know they are **accepted** for who they are—regardless of what they have done or what has happened to them.

What Determines Your Friends' Worth?

If your friends feel they are worth something, they are more likely to feel accepted. But what determines self-worth for many students?

True or False:
A Person's Worth Is Determined by How He or She Looks

Do those around you tend to judge a person's worth based on looks? Check (✔) either true or false for each statement, depending on how people you know would respond.

❑ **True** ❑ **False** Clothes make a big difference to most people.

❑ **True** ❑ **False** Most students feel a lot better when they are wearing really cool stuff.

❑ **True** ❑ **False** Kids at school tend to look down on those who wear "dorky" or "scummy" clothes.

❑ **True** ❑ **False** Really good-looking students tend to get dates easier.

❑ **True** ❑ **False** The person who said, "Looks aren't everything" was probably ugly!

To some people, *image* is everything. Do you agree or disagree with that perspective? Why?

_____

_____

_____

_____

True or False:
A Person's Worth Is Determined by What He or She Has

Do those around you tend to judge a person's worth based on power, personality, or possessions? Check (✔) either true or false for each statement, depending on how you think most people would respond.

❑ **True** ❑ **False** A big spender always seems to have plenty of friends.

❑ **True** ❑ **False** People who have outgoing and perky personalities seem to get elected to class office.

❑ **True** ❑ **False** A student who is ugly, poor, or has zero personality is rarely chosen homecoming king or queen.

❑ **True** ❑ **False** Status, personality, and possessions make a difference with the "in crowd."

To some people, *what you have* is everything. Do you agree or disagree with this perspective? Why?

_____

_____

_____

_____

True or False:
A Person's Worth Is Determined by What He or She Does

Do those around you tend to judge a person's worth based on performance? Check (✔) either true or false for each statement below, depending on how people you know would respond.

❑ True ❑ False Straight-A students are more highly respected than D students.

❑ True ❑ False Most people believe "Winning isn't everything; it's the only thing."

❑ True ❑ False A school doesn't have parades or assemblies in honor of the losing team.

❑ True ❑ False Students today feel a lot of pressure to perform—get good grades, do well at sports, be all they can be, etc.

❑ True ❑ False Students feel that most people accept them based on how well they perform.

To some people *performance* is everything. Do you agree or disagree with that perspective? Why?

_____

_____

_____

_____

Acceptance and Worth

Underline the sentence that best describes what you think *accepting others* should mean.

1. Accepting others means welcoming the richest and most popular kids into your clique.
2. Accepting others means approving of everything another person does whether it's legal or illegal, moral or immoral.
3. Accepting others means accepting people for who they are, regardless of what they have, how they look, or what they do.
4. Accepting others means recognizing a person as worthy if they measure up to your standard of performance.

If you underlined sentence number 3, you selected a good description of acceptance. **Acceptance says, "You are worth being accepted just for who you are."**

Good looks and cool clothes may get you noticed. Having a lot of stuff may cause some people to like you. And your accomplishments may gain you the approval of others. But you shouldn't allow image, possessions, or performance to determine your worth as a person. Nor should you judge the worth of your friends by how they look, what they have, or what they do.

Our worth as individuals was determined long before any of us could begin to boast of good looks, possessions, or accomplishments.

Your Worth Was Determined before You Were Born

Read Genesis 1:26-27.

In whose image were you created? _____

Think about this for a moment. God knows everything there is to know, has all the power in the universe, and can accomplish anything and everything He wants to accomplish. And He chose to create you in His image. How does that make you feel? Check (✔) any words that apply.

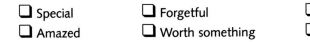

❑ Special   ❑ Forgetful   ❑ Bloated
❑ Amazed   ❑ Worth something   ❑ Lonesome

And what does God think of His human creation?

"What is man that you are mindful of him, the son of man that you care for him? You made him a little lower than the heavenly beings and crowned him with glory and honor" (Ps. 8:4–5 NIV).

God thinks enough about His human creation to crown us with what?

_____ and _____

"But wait just a minute," you say. "Crowned with glory and honor? I know of people, even students like me, who have cheated, lied, and hurt other people. Some students have even murdered their own classmates! Are they still considered God's worthy creation?"

God's human creation has fallen a long way from His crown of glory and honor. Every person born after Adam and Eve has sinned and fallen short of God's glory (see Rom. 3:23). But consider how valuable God's fallen creation still is to Him.

"For you know that God paid a ransom to save you from the empty life you inherited from your ancestors" (1 Pet. 1:18).

How much ransom do you think God paid for His human creation, which has fallen short of His glory?

1. 100 billion dollars   2. 100 trillion dollars
3. 100 zillion dollars   4. Other? _____

"And the ransom he paid was not in mere gold and silver. He paid for you with the precious lifeblood of Christ, the sinless, spotless Lamb of God" (1 Pet.1:18–19).

What is your worth to God? You are *WORTH JESUS* to God, because that is what He paid for you. As payment to ransom you, God sent His only Son to earth to die on the cross in your place.

If you had been the only person God ever created, God would have sent His Son to die for you. And if you *were* the only person ever created, what person would have nailed Jesus Christ to the cross? _____

God settled it. You are worth something very precious to God, and so are your friends. This means that as a 911 friend, you can accept others for who they are regardless of how they look, what they have, or what they do. Why? Because your friends are of infinite value and worth to Creator God—so much so that they are worth Jesus!

Prayer

Take a moment to tell God how thankful you are that you and your friends are worth Jesus to Him.

_____

_____

_____

_____

_____

_____

_____

_____

Discovery Day

At breakfast, Jenny Shaw's cabin won the camp director's "Mr. Clean" award for the third straight day. Heather Wells led the cheers—as usual—while Ann stayed in the background—as usual. Most people couldn't believe that Ann and Heather were friends. Heather was so outgoing, and Ann was so shy. And yet Heather never left Ann out of anything. That was another reason why Ann appreciated her best friend.

After breakfast, Ann and Heather went to their favorite log next to the archery range for devotions. Before they could open their Bibles, Ann brought up the topic that had been in the front of her brain since their brief, middle-of-the-night chat. "Before we read, I have to apologize to you."

Heather cocked her head with curiosity. "For what?"

Ann squirmed on the log, feeling very nervous about bringing up the subject. "Last night I told you that I didn't have any problems with my grandpa."

"Yeah, because your grandfather died two years ago."

"Well, I didn't exactly tell you the truth about Grandpa."

"You mean about him being dead?"

"No, I mean about the problems."

"You had problems with your grandfather? That's what the dream was about last night?"

The fresh reminder about the dream sent a chill down Ann's spine. She stared at the ground, pushing pine needles around with the toe of her sandal. Finally she said, "I've never told anyone about this, Heather—not even my parents."

Heather took Ann's hand. She seemed to sense how difficult the issue was for Ann to talk about. "It's OK, Annie," she assured her friend. "You know I'm here for you. You can tell me if you want to."

"It all started when I was about four years old. My parents would take me to stay with Grandma and Grandpa Bennett several weekends a year while they went away. When Grandma was asleep or at the store, my grandpa . . . did things to me . . . that weren't right." Ann could not keep tears of shame from flooding her eyes. "He . . . touched me in my private areas. He made me . . . touch him too. He said it was our secret. He said I could never tell anyone, so I never did. But I can't stop dreaming about it."

Resting her head on her friend's shoulder, Ann began to cry. She felt Heather's comforting arm around her and heard her friend sniffling too. "Annie, you poor thing," Heather said in a broken voice. "I didn't know you had such a big hurt in your past. I'm so sorry." The two of them sat and cried for a while.

"How long did this go on?" Heather said as they wiped their eyes dry.

"About three years," Ann explained. "Then Grandpa got real sick. He was in a nursing home until he died two years ago."

"I didn't tell my parents," Ann continued, "because I thought I would get in trouble. I thought it was my fault."

"Annie, you were only a little kid," Heather argued. "It wasn't your fault. Your grandfather was wrong. Nobody should do those things to a child."

"Then why do I feel so guilty about what happened?"

Heather thought for a moment. "I don't know, but maybe Jenny does." Jenny Shaw was their counselor at camp this week. Both girls thought of Jenny as a spiritual big sister.

"I don't know if I can tell Jenny about this," Ann said, frowning at the thought.

"I'm glad you told me about your dreams and your grandfather, Annie," Heather assured. "I'm going to be with you and pray with you through this. But I think it would be good to ask Jenny's advice about how to handle this. We could talk to her together."

Ann winced, but somehow she knew Heather was right. Jenny Shaw had been a great source of spiritual strength since Ann came into the youth group. "Maybe Jenny won't have time to talk," Ann argued weakly.

"You just tell me that you're ready to talk to her," Heather said, "and I'll do the rest."

As difficult as it had been for her to tell Heather her dark secret, Ann already felt better for doing so. It was like Heather had taken some of the burden just by listening to her and crying with her. If talking to Jenny could help her feel even better, Ann could do it. "OK," she said, "I'd like to talk to Jenny—if you will go with me."

Heather smiled an encouraging smile. "You got it. That's what friends are for."

Your 911 Response

You may not know someone in Ann's situation, but many of your friends may be crying out for acceptance because they suffer from a low sense of self-worth. They often mistakenly believe that their value, worth, and dignity as persons is determined by their appearance, their accomplishments, their influence on others, or their past or present experiences.

The Signs of Low Self-Worth

How can you tell if a friend is suffering from a low sense of self-worth and feelings of false guilt? There are at least four signs that will help you discover if your friend feels less than acceptable to himself or herself and to others.

The "I'm-Unattractive" Syndrome

Some of your friends may feel that their worth is attached to how they look, and they see themselves as a 1 or 2 on a scale of 10. Do any of these comments reflect how some of your friends feel?

- "My feet are so big I don't need skis!"
- "My complexion's so bad even my zits have zits!"
- "My clothes are so out of date my grandma raids my closet."
- "I look like I've been dropped in a vat of ugly."

Do you know people, perhaps in your own youth group, who feel negative about their appearance?

❏ Yes   ❏ No   ❏ I do

The "I'm-a-Failure" Syndrome

Some of your friends may feel that their worth is determined by what they do and how well they do it, and they feel like they can't do anything well. Can you think of friends who might feel like this?

- "No matter how hard I try, I can't make straight A's."
- "I love sports, but I'm nothing but a klutz on the field."
- "I'm the world's worst at operating a computer."
- "Everything I touch turns to mud."

Do you know one or two of your friends who might feel that they are failures at what they want to do?

❑ **Yes**　　❑ **No**　　❑ **I do**

The "I'm-a-Nobody" Syndrome

Do some of your friends feel unimportant and unneeded? Can you think of anyone who may have said something like this?

- "Why can't I ever get elected as a class officer?"
- "Nobody wants to come to *my* parties."
- "I'm always the last one chosen for a team."
- "If I didn't show up for school, I don't think anyone would miss me."

Do some of your friends tend to feel like nobodies?

❑ **Yes**　　❑ **No**　　❑ **I do**

The "It's-My-Fault" Syndrome

Like Ann in the story, some of your friends may suffer from feelings of false guilt because of the things that have happened to them. Do you know people who might feel like this?

- "We just broke up. I guess I just can't keep a boyfriend/girlfriend."
- "My parents aren't getting along, and I think it's my fault."
- "My folks say money is tight, so I figure I'm a drain on their finances."
- "I wasn't invited to the party, but I have no one to blame but myself."

Do some of your friends tend to blame themselves for what has happened to them?

❑ **Yes**　　❑ **No**　　❑ **I do**

Helping Your Friends See with God's 20/20 Vision

Some of your friends may feel unattractive, unsuccessful, unimportant, or responsible for bad things. You may even experience some of those feelings. While these feelings are real, they do not reflect what is really true.

Any time we judge our self-worth based on appearance, possessions, or performance, we cloud the true picture of who we really are. Why? The answer is found in the sentence below. Choose one word from each column to fill in the blanks correctly.

(a)	(b)	(c)
Schools	the laboratory	an animal
God	their minds	His Son
Parents	His image	an angel

"(a) _____ has already determined my worth by creating me in (b)_____ _____ and confirmed that worth by sending (c) _____ _____ to die for me."

You and your friends need to **see yourselves as God sees you—no more and no less.** How? By accepting yourself and others as the valued people you are.

Prayer

Write your prayer to God, telling Him you want Him to work through you this week to confirm your friendship partner's true worth as a unique person created in His image by *accepting him or her for who he or she is.*

_____

_____

_____

_____

_____

_____

_____, Amen.

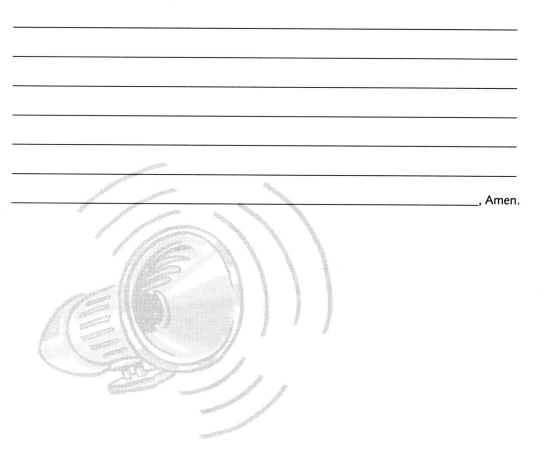

Heather asked Jenny Shaw to meet with them during free time right after lunch, and she agreed. They met in the cabin while their four other roommates were horseback riding.

With Heather holding her hand for encouragement, Ann told Jenny about her dreams and the dark events from her childhood. Jenny asked her all the "who," "where," and "when" questions without pushing her to go into graphic details. Ann couldn't keep from crying as she talked, but Heather and Jenny were right there for her. "It's OK to cry, Ann," Jenny encouraged, holding her. "Just let it all out. We're here for you." The tears flowed freely for all three of them.

When the emotions subsided, Jenny said, "There is a term for what happened to you during those so-called 'secret visits' with your grandfather. Do you know what it is, Ann?"

Ann knew what Jenny was getting at. But she hesitated, because it sounded so dirty, so terrible. "Yes, I know," she admitted finally.

"Then tell me in your own words exactly what your grandfather did to you during your secret visits," Jenny pressed.

They seemed like forbidden words to Ann, just like swearing or using God's name in vain. She didn't want to say them. But with Jenny's gentle prodding, she did. "Grandpa . . . sexually abused me."

"That's right, Ann," Jenny affirmed. "It's very important that you understand that. Parents and grandparents and other adults are supposed to care for you and to protect you. No matter how loving he may have seemed at other times, your grandfather took something from you for his own pleasure, and that's abuse. Sexual abuse is a crime, Ann. If your grandfather were still alive and abusing you like that today, I would insist that you go to the police or a child-protection agency. It's that serious."

"But it was partly my fault," Ann interjected, fighting back tears again. "Grandpa used to say I was too cute to resist."

Jenny slowly shook her head. "It was *not* your fault, Ann. No matter what your grandpa told you, no matter how guilty he made you feel, you are not to blame."

Ann felt something very freeing in Jenny's words, like another large weight had been lifted from her shoulders. "It wasn't my fault," she repeated.

"That's right," Jenny said, smiling. "And I also want you to know that I am proud of you for the courage it takes to face all this. I love you and care about you, Ann. I want to help you heal from the terrible inner wound you suffered."

"Heal?" Ann wondered aloud. "But it was a long time ago."

"Let me explain," Jenny said. "Suppose you broke your arm but never told anybody about it and never went to the doctor to get it set. What would happen?"

"The arm would probably get better, but it might be crooked," Ann guessed. "Or it might not get better at all."

"You're right," Jenny said. "And something like that has happened to you. You were emotionally wounded as a child because of your grandfather's abuse. Your emotions may have healed a little with time. But now God can involve others that care about you to help mend the emotional part of you that has been hurting for so long."

That made sense to Ann. "I see," she said.

"So I want you to know that I'm going to be with you as the healing takes place. You can count on me, Ann."

"Me too," Heather chimed in.

Jenny glanced at her watch. "But it's time for team games down on the field right now. I would like to meet here again tomorrow if you two are willing. There are some other things about your abuse we need to talk about."

"I'd like that," Ann said eagerly. Heather agreed to be there too.

Before leaving the cabin, Jenny led the girls in a tender prayer for Ann's healing. All through the day Ann felt brighter and happier inside. She had revealed the darkest blot from her past, and two people who meant the world to her still accepted her. Ann sensed that today was the beginning of a new chapter in her life.

Your 911 Response

Ann is beginning to realize that Heather and Jenny accept her regardless of what happened in her past. Ann realizes that her two friends are able to separate her past from who she is as a person. Of course, in Ann's case, she did absolutely nothing wrong. But true acceptance separates what a person *does* from who he or she is.

Imagine that your school has reached the final game of the volleyball championships, and you are excited to be part of the team. One more win, and your team is number one. The game starts badly for you, as you serve the ball out of bounds. From there, things just get worse, and you can't believe how poorly you are playing. With the game on the line, you again serve the ball out of bounds. The other team takes quick advantage of your mistake and wins the game—and the championship.

As you sit stunned on the bench after the game, you expect the worst from your teammates for almost single-handedly giving away the championship. Several of them say nothing to you. A couple of them come by to say something like, "Tough luck" or "We'll get them next year." One bitter teammate communicates her disappointment by flashing you the "choke" sign. Nobody is happy about how you played, and it sure shows. You couldn't feel worse.

Then another teammate sits down beside you. "I just want you to know that I really enjoyed playing volleyball with you this year," she begins. "Your positive attitude through the season has helped me stay focused. And it was great getting to know you better. I hope we can play together next year. You're really special." Then, after a friendly pat on the shoulder, she leaves.

For a brief moment, you forget about the agony of defeat. This teammate didn't say anything about how poorly you played (or, for that matter, how well you played in other games). She just showed her interest in you for being you!

Can you think of an experience in which someone accepted you for who you were—apart from what you did or failed to do?   ❏ **Yes**   ❏ **No**

If yes, briefly describe the experience here. What was the occasion? What did this person say or do to communicate acceptance apart from what you did or didn't do?

_____

_____

_____

The Difference between Acceptance and Approval

Do you agree or disagree with the following statements?

❏ **Agree**   ❏ **Disagree**   What the Nazi leader, Adolph Hitler, did in ordering the killing of millions of Jews during World War II was unacceptable.

❏ **Agree**   ❏ **Disagree**   The murderous rampage of Eric Harris and Dylan Klebold, killing twelve students and one teacher at Colombine High School in 1999, was unacceptable.

Did you agree that the killing of Jewish people was unacceptable? Yes, it was wrong and we should not approve of it.

Did you agree that the actions of Harris and Klebold were unacceptable? Yes, what they did was wrong and unacceptable behavior.

But do the horrible actions of these three persons make them unworthy of Christ dying for them?

❏ **Yes**   ❏ **No**   ❏ **Not sure**

God makes a distinction between acceptance and approval.
God's acceptance says, "You are worth being redeemed—you are worth Jesus."
God's approval says, "I am pleased with you."

Murder is wrong, and God is not pleased with anyone who murders. But even though God does not *approve* of murderous actions, he can still *accept* people who murder because they are worth being redeemed. Despite their horrible deeds, Hitler, Harris, and Klebold are still worth Jesus. Had any one of them been the only person created, Christ still would have died for him.

"Your iniquities [sins] have separated you from your God" (Isa. 59:2 NIV).

What separates us from God? _____

God does disapprove of our sins, but at the same time he finds us worthy of saving. Read Micah 7:18, 19 below. God makes a distinction between you and your unacceptable behavior. Notice that He separates you from your sin. What does He do with your sin?

_____

_____

_____

"Where is another God like you, who pardons the sin of the survivors among his people? . . . You will trample our sins under your feet and throw them into the depth of the ocean" (Micah 7:18–19).

What you do is *not* the same as who you are, otherwise God in Christ could not separate you from your sin and throw those sins away. God in Christ can accept us for who we are without approving of what we do.

Be Aware of Today's Cultural Mind-set

Have you ever heard these views expressed?

❏ Yes   ❏ No   "You are judging me when you say that what I do is wrong just because you believe it is wrong."

❏ Yes   ❏ No   "If you say homosexuality is wrong for everyone, you're actually being intolerant."

❏ Yes   ❏ No   "You are free to believe differently than others, but don't criticize people for the way they live, because that's acting like a bigot."

❏ Yes   ❏ No   "You are putting people down when you are critical of the way they live their lives."

Each of the above statements expresses a fundamental cultural mind-set. Check (✔) the statement that best expresses this mind-set:

1. Give peace a chance.
2. Who I am is wrapped up in what I do, what I think, and what I believe.
3. Just do it.

Much of today's culture wrongly claims that who you are equals what you do. Acceptance and approval are one and the same to them. The Bible teaches otherwise. God's Word tells us that who you are is separate from what you do. When one of your friends mistakenly ties his or her sense of value and worth to what he or she thinks, believes, or does, your friend will feel personally rejected if you disapprove of his or her beliefs and actions. But remember, God in Christ can love and accept people for who they are without approving of what they do. By demonstrating Christlike acceptance, we can show our friends that we value them for who they are without approving of their immoral actions or lifestyles. We will explore how to do that in our next Discovery Day.

NOTE: Contact your Friendship Partner today or tomorrow and set up your meeting time to walk through Discovery Day Five together.

Prayer

Thank God that He separates what you do from who you are. Thank Him that He finds you worth Jesus and has cast your sins into the sea of His forgetfulness. Right now tell God how you feel about these truths.

_____

_____

_____

A 911 Friend Is Accepting

ANN'S STORY CONTINUES

Ann, what have you been thinking and feeling since our time yesterday?" Jenny Shaw was sitting on one bunk; Ann and Heather were on the bunk facing her. Their four roommates were down at the lake, water skiing and tubing.

"*Mixed* would be a good word," Ann said. "A few bad flashbacks have popped into my mind without warning. And some of the old feelings came along with them—you know, feeling dirty, scared, ashamed. But at other times I thought about our talk yesterday and was really glad that somebody knows what I went through. I tried to push away the bad thoughts and feelings and concentrate on the good ones. A couple of times, when I felt like crying, I tried to think happy thoughts."

"Don't push away the sad stuff too hard, Ann," Jenny admonished in a loving tone. "One of the worst things you can do at this time is try to deny or forget what happened to you or to keep your emotions bottled up inside. The best things you can do are to admit what has happened, to recognize and express your feelings, and to accept the help of others. I think it would be good for you to see a Christian counselor if your parents will consent to it."

Ann felt an electric shock of fear. "My parents? You're not going to tell my parents about this, are you?"

Jenny reached out a hand to touch Ann gently on the arm. "It may be hard for you, but you need to tell your parents about the sexual abuse. They are important to your healing."

"But what if Mom freaks out? Grandpa was her father."

"She will probably need a lot of help to get through it too," Jenny explained. "But she loves you, and I'm sure she wants to help you get through your pain, even if it is painful for her."

Ann felt butterflies in her stomach. "How do I break this news to my parents?"

"We can talk about that before we go home on Saturday, Ann," Jenny assured. "But I'll go with you when you tell them—if you want me to."

"I can be there too, Annie," Heather put in, "if you need somebody to lean on."

Ann's butterflies didn't all go away, but they quieted down some. "You two would really go with me?"

"I'm glad to be there for you," Jenny said.

"I don't want you to be alone during such a tough time," Heather added. "If you want me there, I'm there."

Ann felt a little teary again at the expression of Jenny's and Heather's closeness. "This isn't easy for me," she said. "I'll take all the help I can get." Heather gave her a big hug.

Then Jenny said, "Ann, I want to encourage you to take advantage of your most important resource for handling everything you're dealing with right now. That resource is God Himself. I want you to know that God does not look down on you because you have been sexually abused. He knows it wasn't your fault. He's not disappointed or mad at you because of how you were treated by your grandfather. I want you to see how God really feels about you. Get your Bibles."

Ann and Heather went to their bunks and

pulled their Bibles out of their suitcases. Jenny told Ann to look up Isaiah 63:9. "Ann, your verse tells us something about how God feels about your pain. Why don't you read it for us."

Ann read aloud. "'In all their distress he too was distressed, and the angel of his presence saved them. In his love and mercy he redeemed them; he lifted them up and carried them all the days of old.'"

"According to this verse, how does God feel when His people are distressed?" Jenny quizzed.

"He feels distressed too," Ann answered.

"So how do you think God feels about what you have been through, Ann?"

"I'm sad and upset about it, so I guess He's sad and upset with me."

Jenny leaned closer. "And how does that make you feel?"

Ann paused to think about it. "If He hurts because I'm hurting, it makes me feel very special, like He really knows me and loves me."

"That's right, Ann," Jenny emphasized. "God knows all about you. He knows how much pain your grandfather's abuse has caused over the years. And He hurts because you hurt. It will help you to remember that."

"My verse is really encouraging too," Heather said.

Jenny nodded and asked Heather to read Matthew 11:28.

"'Come to me, all you who are weary and burdened, and I will give you rest,'" Heather read.

Jenny looked at Ann. "Do you feel 'weary and burdened' from the dark secret you have carried since your grandfather abused you?"

"That's one way to put it," Ann said.

"According to this verse, what does Jesus have to offer for your condition?"

Ann glanced at the verse in Heather's Bible then looked back at Jenny. "Rest," she answered with a slight smile.

"There's one more passage I want you to see, Ann." Jenny directed them to Hebrews 4:15–16.

Heather volunteered to read aloud while Ann followed along in her Bible. "'For we do not have a high priest who is unable to sympathize with our weaknesses, but we have one who has been tempted in every way, just as we are—yet was without sin. Let us then approach the throne of grace with confidence, so that we may receive mercy and find grace to help us in our time of need.'"

"God not only feels my hurt and offers rest, He can help me," Ann answered before Jenny asked the question.

"That's so important to understand, Ann," Jenny said. "God is willing and waiting to help you get through your tough time. So one of the best things you can do to cope with your feelings is to cultivate a deeper relationship with God and depend on Him for strength and help."

Ann dropped her head. "I haven't been doing too well in that category. This helps me to want to get back to having my personal devotions again."

"That's good, Ann," Jenny responded. "Spending time each day in prayer and Bible reading will help you receive the loving acceptance and rest God has promised you."

Your 911 Response

In the previous Discovery Days, you learned that God accepts you for who you are and that you are to accept others as He does.

"So accept each other just as Christ has accepted you; then God will be glorified" (Rom. 15:7).

You may be asking, "How do I accept others like Christ accepts me? And how do I receive this kind of acceptance from others?" Let's find out.

Ann is about to discover how to receive God's loving acceptance. You may not have been sexually abused as a child, but you still may struggle at feeling accepted by others, and you may find it hard to express acceptance to others. A lot of people tend to struggle to maintain a healthy sense of self-worth and to show true acceptance to others.

The Way Christ Accepts Us

You understand now that Christ accepts people for who they are. But are there certain conditions to His acceptance?

Complete the following sentence by checking (✔) the statement you believe is most correct.

"Christ's acceptance of us . . .

_____ . . . has to be earned with good works on our part."

_____ . . . will be withdrawn if we don't believe in Him by age twenty-one."

_____ . . . is a loving acceptance without conditions."

Read Romans 5:6–8 below, then fill in the missing words in the sentences that follow.

"When we were utterly helpless, Christ came . . . and died for us sinners . . . But God showed his great love for us by sending Christ to die for us while we were still sinners" (Rom. 5:6–8).

"When we were _____ _____ Christ came . . . and died for us sinners . . . But God showed his great love for us by sending Christ to die for us while we were _____ _____."

"Utterly helpless" means we are unable to do anything to earn our acceptance in Christ. The fact that Christ died for us while we were "still sinners" means His loving acceptance is without condition.

Christ's loving acceptance is both unearned and without conditions.

Christ's acceptance can't approve of my sins, right?

In John 8, Jesus was called by the religious leaders to judge a woman caught in the act of adultery. They wanted to stone her to death. He said, "All right, stone her. But let those who have never sinned throw the first stone" (John 8:7).

Does this mean that Jesus approved of the woman's immorality?

❏ Yes   ❏ No   ❏ Not Sure

All the religious leaders slipped away, then Jesus asked the woman, "Where are your accusers? Didn't even one of them condemn you?" The woman answered, "No, Lord." Then Jesus said, "Neither do I. Go and sin no more" (vv. 10–11).

The woman had clearly done sinful things, but Jesus didn't condemn her. Why? How can

Jesus be so accepting? Check (✔) **two** answers below that you think fit with the Bible verses in today's lesson:

❑ Jesus just refuses to believe that people are as bad as others think.

❑ Jesus doesn't excuse sin, but His love for people enables Him to look beyond their faults and see their need for salvation.

❑ Jesus believes it doesn't matter what a person does, because sin is only sin if a person thinks it's sin.

❑ Jesus isn't interested in overlooking sin, but He *is* interested in forgiving the person who sins.

Christ accepts you for who you are, regardless of what you have done. He doesn't excuse your sins, but His forgiving heart enables Him to look beyond your faults and see your need for salvation. You are freely forgiven because of Christ's sacrificial death.

"He is so rich in kindness that he purchased our freedom through the blood of his Son, and our sins are forgiven" (Eph 1:7).

God doesn't overlook our sins or approve of them, but thanks to Christ's death on the cross, God can forgive us. God so loved you and the world that He gave his only Son to provide for the forgiveness of your sin. Read John 3:16.

The Power to Accept Lovingly as Christ Accepts

Christ's loving acceptance is our example. By loving our friends as Christ loves us, we can look beyond our friends' unacceptable behavior and accept them for who they are.

"Most important of all, continue to show deep love for each other, for love covers a multitude of sins" (1 Pet. 4:8).

Your friends need your Christlike acceptance, especially when their self-worth is being tested or they feel rejected or abandoned by others. Others may reject them, but you can be there for them with your loving acceptance.

On an "acceptance scale" of 1 to 10 (with 1 meaning "low need for acceptance" and 10 meaning "high need for acceptance"), how would you rate your friend's need for your acceptance in each of these circumstances?

1. A friend has just learned that she has been made fun of behind her back.
    • My friend rates a _____ in need of my acceptance.
2. A friend got caught taking sports supplies from the school and was kicked off the team permanently.
    • My friend rates a _____ in need of my acceptance.
3. I told a friend of some disappointments I've been going through. He responded with an insensitive, "get over it" kind of attitude.
    • My friend rates a _____ in need of my acceptance.

Did you tend to rate your friend's need for your acceptance higher in #1 than you did in #2 and even lower in #3? It's easier to accept our friends when they have been rejected or unfairly hurt by others. It's more difficult when their problems are the consequences of their wrong choices or when they have actually hurt us. True acceptance means lovingly accepting our friends regardless of the circumstances.

This isn't always easy. So how *do* you get the power to accept your friends when they don't act very "acceptable"? Check (✔) some possible answers from the following:

☐ Repeat "I love you" ten times.　☐ Call 911　　　　　　☐ Read more of the Bible

☐ Go on-line and ask someone　　☐ Pray harder　　　　☐ _____
　 in a chat room.　　　　　　　☐ Meditate

Prayer, Bible reading, and meditation are all helpful. But we get the power to accept others through a biblical principle: Give out of God's supply.

Read this verse thoughtfully:

"We love each other as a result of his loving us first" (1 John 4:19).

What do you think this verse means? Is your power to love others really based on God loving you first? How? Why?

_____

_____

_____

This verse puts the command to accept each other as Christ has accepted us in a new light. The way Christ accepts you is not just a guideline for you to follow. You are actually empowered to accept others lovingly as a result of Christ lovingly accepting you first. In other words, the way you receive loving acceptance from God is the way you are able to give loving acceptance to others.

Confirm the Schedule with Your Friendship Partner

My scheduled time to go over Discovery Day Five with my Friendship Partner is _____

_____ (day, place, and time).

Discovery Day Five will walk you both through an exercise that will help you share with each other the kind of acceptance you have received from God. You will probably be amazed at how much acceptance God will empower you to give!

Prayer

End this Discovery Day with a prayer of thanks to God for thinking of you as His ministry partner and for wanting to involve you in His ministry of accepting others.

_____

_____

_____

A 911 Friend Is Accepting

ANN'S STORY CONTINUES

When Jenny Shaw arrived at the Cassidy home late Sunday afternoon, Ann introduced her to her parents, Jerry and Dorothy. Heather Wells was already there. Ann had told her parents only that Jenny wanted to chat with them about some topics that came up at camp last week.

"We had a great time at camp, Mr. and Mrs. Cassidy," Jenny began. "And I really enjoyed being with your daughter and the other girls. Ann is a delightful girl, and I love her like a younger sister." Jerry and Dorothy beamed with pride.

"We go to camp each summer to have a good time," Jenny continued. "But spending a week together also gives the students an extended opportunity to talk about the more serious side of life, such as their struggles and problems. Don't worry: Ann isn't in any kind of trouble. But last week she talked to me—and Heather—about something very hurtful in her life. I encouraged her to share it with you. Heather and I are here mainly to provide moral support. Go ahead, Ann."

Ann wanted to roll up into a ball and hide just as she had when her grandfather came into her room at night years ago. Jenny had encouraged her to go ahead even though she was nervous. So she took a deep breath and began. "Mom and Dad, do you remember the times you left me at Grandpa and Grandma Bennett's when you went away for the weekend?"

Jerry nodded, and Dorothy said, "Yes, your grandparents always loved having you come over. It was just before Grandpa got sick. You were about five or six at the time."

Ann forced herself to go on. "Well, something happened while I was staying with them. It happened several times, and I never told you about it." Ann paused and bit her lip. "I . . . I was sexually abused by Grandpa Bennett."

The expression of shock on her parents' faces was severe. "What?" her dad exclaimed in disbelief.

Ann remembered Jenny urging her to state clearly what had happened. "For about three years, Grandpa Bennett sexually abused me when I stayed at their house. He made me keep it a secret."

Ann glanced at her mother just as the woman began to dissolve into tears. Clasping a hand to her mouth, she said repeatedly, "Oh no, oh no." Ann's father seemed to have turned to stone with a look of horror etched on his face.

Ann pressed on. "I never told anyone about it because I was embarrassed and scared. But I have had nightmares about what happened ever since. At camp, I had another terrible dream. So I told Heather and Jenny about the abuse. Jenny said I should tell you, even though we knew it would be hard. I really need your help to get through this."

"Why didn't you tell us, Ann?" Jerry said with sadness in his voice.

"I was afraid, Dad. I thought it was partly my fault, and I didn't want to get into trouble. Besides, Grandpa said it was our little secret, and I believed him."

Silence fell on the room like a suffocating

Discovery Day

5

blanket. Ann's mother cried softly, and her father sat in silence, stunned and hurt. Ann dabbed a few tears from her eyes as she watched her parents process the shocking news. Heather and Jenny sat and prayed silently.

Finally, Jerry Cassidy got up from his chair and approached his daughter. Kneeling down in front of her, he said with large tears forming in his eyes, "Sweetheart, I'm so sorry I wasn't there to protect you from the abuse. You didn't deserve it. It wasn't your fault. I hurt so deeply for you because I love you so much." Then he enveloped Ann in his arms, and they sobbed together. In seconds, Dorothy joined them. Jenny and Heather watched while blinking away tears.

After a few minutes, Jenny stood and said, "I'm sure there are many things you want to talk about together, so we will leave you alone. I suggested to Ann that the three of you consider seeing a Christian counselor together. Perhaps Pastor O'Neill can recommend someone in the community."

"That's a good idea," Jerry said, standing and wiping tears from his face with a handkerchief.

"Ann, as well as both of you, are going to need some time to heal from this deep emotional wound," Jenny continued. "Each of you will need all the love and acceptance and support you can receive. Doug and I are available to help any way we can. And Ann is blessed to have such an accepting friend like Heather. In time, I know God will help Ann and both of you to heal from the awful things that happened."

Jenny led the small group in a brief prayer. Then she and Heather hugged the Cassidys good-bye. As they moved toward the door, Ann came with them. "Thank you so much for being here with me," she said. "I don't think I could have done it without you."

Your 911 Response

Heather and Jenny have been good 911 friends to Ann. They are learning how to accept others lovingly because they understand very specifically how they have been accepted by God.

Receive in Order to Give

Walk through this exercise with your friendship partner.

Here is the key principle: As we receive from God, He empowers us to give to others. Obviously, it is difficult to give what you don't have. This exercise will help you and your friend realize and appreciate how God has accepted you so you can share that same kind of acceptance with each other.

"We love each other as a result of his loving us first" (1 John 4:19).

There are many dimensions of Christ's acceptance of us, but we will focus on three of them from Luke 7 and Ephesians 4.

I. A. Receive Christ's Acceptance—He Loves You without Conditions, Regardless of What You Have Done

Think of some things you have done that were clearly wrong, things perhaps you are ashamed of. Regardless of what you did, Christ loves you so much that He died for you. Christ didn't say He would love *if* you do this or *because* you do that. He loves you, *period*—without any conditions. Write down how you feel knowing that Christ wraps His arms around you and says, "I love you no matter what you have done or haven't done."

_____

_____

_____

_____

Take turns expressing to each other what you have written down.

I. B. Give Christlike Acceptance without Judging Another's Motives

"Stop judging others, and you will not be judged" (Matt. 7:1).

Christlike acceptance means that we do not condemn or judge another person's motives. A friend may do something that hurts you, but by God's grace you won't hold a grudge or be critical. Rather, in loving-kindness you will always think the best.

Take turns with your friend repeating aloud this acceptance pledge.

"Because I receive Christ's acceptance, by His help I will not judge you if you do something I don't appreciate, nor will I hold a critical attitude if you should hurt me. Because Christ loves me without condition, I can, by His power, think the best of you and love you without judging your motives."

_____

(Sign your name here)

"Love thinks the best of others" (See 1 Cor. 13:7).

II. A. Receive Christ's Acceptance
His Love Is Patient and Gentle

Being in Christ is the safest place in the world. If you fall down, He picks you up. If you fall down again, He will pick you up again. Even if you mess up big-time, He doesn't gripe at you. If you suffer, even over the consequences of your wrong choices, He gently suffers with you. Write down how you feel about Christ's patience and gentleness.

_____

_____

_____

Take turns sharing with each other what you have written down.

II. B. Give Christlike Acceptance
Love with Patience, Humility, and Gentleness

"Be humble and gentle. Be patient with each other, making allowance for each other's faults because of your love" (Eph. 4:2).

Christlike, patient acceptance means we are a safe place for our friend—a place that makes allowances for a shortcoming and in loving-kindness accepts our friend, even when what he or she does may hurt us.

Take turns reading aloud this acceptance pledge to each other.

"Because I receive Christ's acceptance, by His help I will be there for you as a safe place in the tough times. Because Christ has accepted me for who I am and is always there for me, I can, by His power, be kind and patient and gentle with you during your tough times."

_____
(Sign your name here)

"Love is patient and kind" (1 Cor. 13:4).

III. A. Receive Christ's Acceptance
He Lovingly Forgives

There is no sin that God cannot forgive. In His heart, God forgives you before you even ask. Christ never holds a grudge or keeps a record of how you have wronged Him. He freely forgives you of anything and everything you might do or say. Write down how you feel about God's loving forgiveness.

_____

_____

_____

_____

Take turns sharing what you have written down.

III. B. Give Christlike Acceptance
Love Others with a Forgiving Heart

"If you forgive others, you will be forgiven" (Luke 6:37).

Christlike acceptance means we have a forgiving heart. Regardless of what others do to us, we forgive them.

Take turns reading aloud this acceptance pledge.

"Because I receive Christ's acceptance, by His help I will forgive those who have done anything wrong to me in the past, in the present, and even in the future. Because Christ accepts and forgives me, I can, by His power, be a forgiving friend to you."

_____
(Sign your name here)

"[Love] keeps no record of when it has been wronged" (1 Cor. 13:5).

Prayer

Close your time in prayer. Commit to God that you will endeavor daily to receive Christ's acceptance and give Christlike acceptance to your friendship partner and to those around you.

The PROJECT 911 Collection

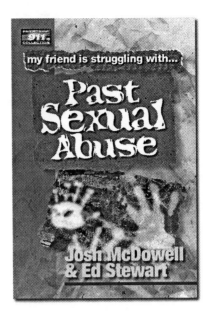

The story of Heather and Ann found in this week's workbook is adapted from the small book entitled *My Friend Is Struggling with Past Sexual Abuse*. The book is designed as a giveaway book that you can read and then give to a friend who has experienced some form of past sexual abuse. Beyond the fictional story, this book provides practical steps a person can take to gain healing and freedom from the pain and false guilt of being sexually abused.

If you want one or more of these books for a friend, contact your youth group leader. He or she may have a number of copies on hand. If not, this and other books in this collection can be ordered in bulk by calling 1-800-933-9673 ext. 9-2039. Or you can purchase copies of this book at your local Christian bookstore.

WEEK THREE

CHAD'S STORY

t's Matty's fault—I just know it is," Chad Rogers hissed aloud to himself. It was dusk as the muscular sophomore marched along the dusty shoulder of the highway in a huff. Chad kicked at an occasional pebble, venting his anger toward his little brother. "He's not even seven years old yet, but Mom treats him like the king of the world. She probably took him to the video store so the little brat could pick out another video game. No wonder she never got to the school to pick me up."

Chad's backpack was slung over one shoulder as he shuffled along. The high school was half a mile behind him, and the Rogerses' country home was still three miles in the distance.

I knew the plan wouldn't work, Chad mumbled to himself. *Mom should have been at the school more than an hour ago—that was the plan. She said she would pick up Rob in town and be at school right after basketball practice. We have to eat supper by 5:30 so Rob and I can get to the church by 6:30. If we aren't there, the youth group will leave for the game without us. Now we won't have time to eat, and we may not even get to the church on time. Matty is going to get it for this.*

The country road was nearly deserted, as usual. But Chad heard a vehicle approaching in the distance behind him. It was probably Mom's van, he figured, but he wasn't about to turn around and look as if he were waiting for it. In fact, Chad decided he would just ignore the van when Mom stopped to pick him up. He would make Matty wait just like she had made him wait at the school. He would just keep walking. His friend Rob, who

was coming with Mom and Matty, would understand. He had a bratty little brother too.

The van slowed behind Chad as he expected. But when it pulled alongside him, it wasn't Mom's dark green van after all. From the corner of his eye, he recognized his dad's pickup truck. "Chad," his dad called out through the open window. Ben Rogers was a supervisor at the local cannery. He had been working ten- to twelve-hour shifts since the middle of summer.

Surprised at his dad's appearance, Chad stopped and turned. "You're home from work kind of early—"

Dad interrupted. "Chad, get in, hurry."

There was something in his voice Chad had never heard before. Dad wasn't angry at him, but he wasn't happy either. He sounded worried, kind of stressed out. *Maybe Mom panicked when she didn't find me at the school,* he thought, *so she called Dad to come look for me.*

Climbing into the truck, he started to explain, but his father cut him off. Putting his hand on his son's shoulder, he said, "Chad, there's been . . . a very bad . . . accident." He was having trouble getting the words out. "We have to get to the hospital . . . right away."

An electric shock of fear shot through Chad. He gripped his dad's arm. "Mom? Matty? Are they all right?"

Ben's chin began to tremble, and his eyes glistened with tears. "It's very bad, son. They all went to the hospital in an ambulance—Mom, Matthew, and Rob too." His voice cracked as he went on. "A big truck crossed the centerline—"

"Dad, no!" Chad yelled, reading the agony in his face. "Not Mom, not Matty, not Rob!

You're wrong. They're coming to pick me up." He turned to look out the back window, hoping to see the van pulling up. The road behind them was deserted.

"Chad, this is a terrible thing, but we have to hold it together and get to the hospital. Mom and Matthew need us now, and Rob needs you too."

Chad buried his face in his hands. "This can't be happening," he said, fighting back the emotions. Then he thought of his older sister who was away at college. "Does Beth know yet? Did you call her?"

"I came straight from work to find you. I'll call Beth when we get to the hospital and find out how Mom and Matty are doing."

"Well then let's hurry, Dad, hurry!" Chad screamed.

Ben pulled the truck into gear, turned it around, and raced back toward town. Feeling the strong, assuring grip on his arm again, Chad heard his dad lift a simple prayer in broken voice, "Help us, Father. Help our family. We need You now."

Please, God, help us, Chad echoed inside.

Arriving in the emergency room, Chad and his father learned that six-year-old Matthew Rogers had died instantly when the large produce truck swerved across the line and hit the Rogerses' van head-on. Chad, Ben, and several other family members sobbed in each other's arms. They were surrounded by a few shocked, grieving neighbors and friends who had raced to the hospital when they heard the news. Also in the circle was Pastor O'Neill from the church that Chad and his family attended.

The hospital's main waiting room was also filling with grieving friends. The youth group's trip to the Friday night high-school football game was canceled when news of the horrible crash reached the church. Several of Chad's and Rob's friends were in the waiting room, comforting each other and praying for the two families. Doug and Jenny Shaw, the youth-group sponsors, were with them.

Chad's emotions took a beating during the first hour at the hospital. The numbing shock of Matty's death was followed by the painful reality that his critically injured mother and friend were still fighting for their lives. The group moved from the emergency room to the surgery waiting room to await news from the surgeons. Each new arrival of relatives to the hospital brought another wave of sorrow and tears to the family. Chad's eyes were red and puffy, and his chest hurt. He could hardly keep his hands from shaking.

Encircled by relatives, Chad had failed to notice that Doug and Jenny Shaw had also come into the surgery waiting room. They approached him and wrapped their arms around him. The three of them stood together for a couple of minutes. The Shaws liked to joke that Chad was their adopted son. Next to his own family, Chad could not think of anyone he loved more as "second parents."

Doug and Jenny led Chad to a small sofa in the corner of the waiting room. Doug handed Chad a small bottle of cold juice he bought from a vending machine down the hall. He thanked him and took a long drink.

"I can't believe what's happening," Chad said fighting back the tears.

"I know it hurts a lot, Chad." Doug's voice choked with emotion. "And we really hurt for you."

"We love you, Chad," Jenny added, "and we wish you didn't have to go through this pain. We're so sorry about Matthew."

"Little Matty is gone, Mom and Rob are hurt badly, and I can't seem to get control of my emotions," Chad moaned.

Doug patted Chad's shoulder. "It's OK. Go ahead and let it all out. We're here to cry with you and your family."

"I know God feels your hurt too, Chad," Jenny said. "If Jesus were here in the flesh right now, I think He would be crying too."

Chad was silent for more than a minute, occasionally wiping a tear from his face. Doug and Jenny sat quietly with him, assuring him with gentle touches. Across the room, Chad's father was being comforted by Pastor O'Neill and a few friends from church. Rob's family was also in the room, huddled with their loved ones. Everyone prayed that the grief they felt over Matthew Rogers's death would not be compounded by the loss of his mother, Margaret, or Chad's friend Rob, who were still in emergency surgery.

"I feel awful about Matty, because I was mad at him," Chad said at last, shaking his head slightly. "I thought he was the reason Mom was late picking me up."

"I know that hurts," Jenny consoled gently.

"I blamed my little brother for something he didn't do," Chad lamented. "It wasn't his fault. Matty died, and I didn't have a chance to apologize for being mad at him."

"We are so sorry you have to deal with those feelings, Chad," Doug said. "We're going to be with you through this."

After several more silent seconds, Chad said, "Mom can't die; she just can't. She's my mom, and I need her. Beth needs her too. God wouldn't take my mom away, would He? And Rob—why did this have to happen to my mom, my best friend, and my little brother? I don't think God is being fair."

Jenny gave Chad another gentle squeeze around the shoulder. "I'm so sorry," she said with quavering voice. "Seeing you hurt makes me hurt."

"I know there are family members who want to be with you," Doug said, "but we want to pray for you right now, OK?" Chad nodded meekly.

The three huddled closely together and linked hands as Doug prayed.

Your 911 Response

Chad is in a world of hurt right now. Put yourself in his place for a moment. How would you feel if someone very close to you—one of your parents, a brother or sister, or a close friend—were seriously injured or suddenly killed? You may have experienced such a loss. Check (✔) any of the words below that describe how you might feel:

❑ Panicky   ❑ Numb   ❑ Depressed   ❑ Sad
❑ Hurt   ❑ Angry   ❑ Tearful   ❑ Confused
❑ Despondent ❑ Discouraged ❑ Controlled   ❑ Calm

You don't often hear about a friend who has suffered a loss as devastating as Chad's—the sudden or violent death of a parent, sibling, or friend. But your friends more often experience other kinds of painful losses— a broken or strained relationship, a romantic breakup, a family separation or divorce, or a move to another state— and these emotional strains can also be intense. Then there are the losses and disappointments of everyday life, such as losing a textbook, failing a test, losing a sporting event, or getting cut from a team. Most of these experiences are not serious, world-shattering losses, but they still hurt. What can a 911 friend do or be to ease the pain and hurt?

What Is Needed to Ease the Hurt

What are some things you can do when a friend experiences some kind of loss or deep disappointment? Fill in the blanks with a word to complete these sentences below that might help.

1. Be an available _____.

2. Speak _____ of encouragement.

3. Offer up _____ to God.

4. Do acts of _____.

5. Have them read _____ passages.

NOTE: The correct words are printed upside down.

1. friend; 2. words; 3. prayers; 4. kindness; 5. Scripture

Being an available friend, of course, is very important. Your encouraging words, prayers, kind deeds, and Scripture sharing are also helpful. Yet God has another way to involve you in easing the grief or trouble of a friend.

Read Matthew 5:4. Then change the following two statements to make them correct.

1. God scolds those who mourn.

_____

2. Those that mourn will be prosecuted.

_____

What does Matthew 5:4 teach? Check (✔) whether you agree or disagree with the statements below:

❑ **Agree**   ❑ **Disagree**   Since mourning is a blessing, you should mourn a lot.

❑ **Agree**   ❑ **Disagree**   God has comfort for those who hurt (mourn).

Take a try at defining comfort.

Comfort is... _____

_____

_____

Comfort is actually God's way of helping to relieve the pain in hurting people. *To comfort* literally means "to ease the grief or trouble of another."

This week you will discover how God wants to involve you in His healing ministry of comfort to your friends.

Prayer

Ask God to help you be a comforting 911 friend to someone this week. You may even want to ask Him to allow one of your friends to be a comforting 911 friend to you.

_____

_____

_____

_____

_____

A *911* Friend Is Affirming

CHAD'S STORY CONTINUES

Waiting for the doctors to come out of surgery was torture for Chad and his family. In the meantime, Ben Rogers was torn between the sad task of arranging for his little boy's body to be picked up by the funeral home and the frail hope that his wife would survive her massive injuries. Chad and Ben both talked to Beth on the phone. She said she would get on a flight for home tonight. Chad was surprised at how calm his older sister sounded on the phone.

Then, along with a room full of family and caring friends, they waited. People occasionally said things to Chad, apparently trying to cheer him up: "God must need your little brother in heaven more than we do"; "At least Matthew didn't suffer long"; "You should be thankful that God let you have him for six years"; "Everything will be all right." Chad knew these people meant well, but some of their comments did not make him feel any better. He found himself returning to Doug and Jenny occasionally just to hear them say "We're sorry" and "We're here for you."

Rob's surgeon came out first, and Chad held his breath as he began his report to family and friends. The gruesome details of his friend's life-threatening injuries and surgery made Chad shudder with shock and fear. Rob would be in intensive care for several days. He was on life support and had a fifty/fifty chance for survival. Chad joined Doug and Jenny to pray with Rob's parents.

When the second doctor, a neurosurgeon, walked into the waiting room about twenty minutes later, Chad wanted to run away and hide. If he didn't hear what the doctor said, he might be able to convince himself that his mom was fine, that this hospital nightmare was only about Matty and Rob. But Chad's dad motioned Chad to his side on the sofa and dropped a comforting arm around his shoulders. Chad placed his hand on Doug's arm for support.

The doctor sat on the coffee table and addressed Ben Rogers. "Your wife is out of surgery and holding her own for the moment. But I'm afraid the prognosis is not good. She suffered serious brain damage in the crash, and we did everything we could for her. But she is not breathing on her own and—I'm sorry to say—her brain activity is very weak."

"You mean my mom is brain-dead?" The timid words tumbled out before Chad could stop them. He had studied a little about brain function in health class during spring term. At the time, *brain-dead* seemed so unrelated to his personal life that the words could have been in a foreign language. Now they were horrifyingly real.

The surgeon turned to him. "We're going to monitor your mother's condition closely through the night, so we will have a better idea what we are facing in the morning. I'm not ready to say she is 'brain-dead.' But it doesn't look good. We have done all we can medically, but I also believe in prayer and miracles. The rest is up to the Great Physician."

Chad squeezed his eyes closed to shut out the cruel world assaulting him. Had his father and Doug not been surrounding him at the moment, he might have bolted from the room.

"When can we see her?" Ben asked the doctor, his voice breaking.

"She should be in ICU by now," the doctor said, standing. "She is in a deep coma, but hearing your voices may be a comfort to her. A few of you may go back if you like."

Chad knew he had to go see his mother, but he hesitated at the idea. To Chad, walking through those doors meant that his mother was really in that sterile room connected to all those machines, and he did not want to admit that. Horrible accidents occurred in other people's lives, not in his. Moments later, Chad was walking down a dimly lit hall toward ICU. Pastor O'Neill and Ben Rogers walked ahead. Chad and Doug Shaw followed. Jenny had left after volunteering to pick up Beth at the airport to bring her to the hospital.

When Chad first glimpsed the patient on the bed, he was relieved. It was not his mother. At least it did not look like his mother. The woman's puffy face was a collage of dark blue, purple, crimson, and pasty white. Her head was swathed in a bandage from the sur-gery. Tubes protruding from the mouth and nose further distorted her face. And the sparkling green eyes that Chad knew were covered by swollen, bluish-purple lids. Chad moved closer to confirm the faint hope that this was someone else's mother, not his.

But his dad's reaction told Chad the truth. Ben slipped his hand around his wife's pale, limp hand on the sheet and began talking to her softly, lovingly. After a minute, it was Chad's turn. He moved to the bed to stand beside his father.

Gazing upon the still form, Chad could finally see a resemblance. The shock of hair sticking out of the bandage was his mother's color. The shape of the ear and dimpled chin were also familiar. *I don't want it to be you, Mom, but it* is *you,* he admitted silently.

At this moment there were no tears. Another strong emotion was boiling up inside him as he gazed on the nearly lifeless body. Chad clenched his jaw to keep the sudden, angry words from blurting out of his mouth: *God, why did You let this happen to my mother?*

Your 911 Response

It's obvious that Chad is suffering through a great loss. He needs something to ease his pain; he needs comfort. But what about your friends whose occasional hurts are not as serious as what Chad is experiencing? They too may need comfort. But how does this idea of comfort really work? How does comfort really help hurting people?

Affirming in Good Times and Bad

The way you can help your friends in bad times is the same way you help them in the good times: You identify with what they are going through. You affirm a person's feelings by identifying with his or her feelings. This means you actually feel something of what they feel.

How do you and your friends respond at a school football, basketball, or soccer game when your team scores? Check (✔) the boxes that apply.

1. ☐ All my friends and our team's fans sit quietly and nod slightly in approval.
2. ☐ All those on our side of the field or court scream and cheer with enthusiasm while I sit quietly and nod in approval.

3. ☐ I jump up and down cheering our team on while all those around me stay seated and nod quietly in approval.

4. ☐ Practically everyone on our side of the field or court jumps up simultaneously and screams and cheers with enthusiasm.

There is probably no way you picked sentence 2, right? How could you stay seated when everyone is cheering your team on? But let's imagine you picked sentence 3. Let's say you are a real school sports fan, but you're the only person at the game who shows any enthusiasm. So when your team scores, you are the only one who cheers. Do you jump and scream with the same amount of enthusiasm as you would if everyone around you were yelling like mad?

☐ **Yes**   ☐ **No**

Why or why not? _____

_____

_____

_____

You may be a little embarrassed about going bonkers at a game if nobody else is. Or you may feel self-conscious if others in the crowd react to your enthusiasm with a thumbs-down. Why might you be less enthusiastic in that setting? Because no one is sharing in your enthusiasm. No one is adding to your excitement.

Here's the principle: When other people share in your joy, they multiply your joy. You have probably experienced this principle. For example, when do you laugh the most: when watching a funny movie at home by yourself or when watching a funny movie in a crowded theater where everyone around you is howling with laughter? _____

Why?_____

_____

_____

Joy is contagious. One person's joy sparks and multiplies joy in others nearby. Think about it as a formula that looks like this:

Your Joy x Friend's Joy = More Joy for Friend

Experience Romans 12:15a with a Friend

Try this out. Experience a Scripture verse with your friend today or tomorrow and multiply your friend's joy.

"When others are happy, be happy with them" (Rom. 12:15a).

When you are with a friend ask, "Has anything good happened to you lately?" If the answer is yes, listen carefully to what your friend shares. Then share in your friend's joy. For example, you might say: "Hey, that's great! I'm really happy for you!" or "I feel so good about what happened to you!"

Sharing your friend's joy isn't just about saying words. Being happy with your friend means identifying with his or her joy until you begin to feel joy with your friend.

How Comfort Works

Imagine that you are really bummed out. Your girlfriend broke up with you today, or you just found out that your boyfriend is going out with other girls. You are really hurt. You feel rejected, unwanted, unlovable—things couldn't be worse.

Imagine you get together with your best friend and dump out all your frustration, anger, and feelings of betrayal. Eventually, you explain just how much it all hurts. Describe how you would feel in the following situations:

3. Your friend zonks out and goes to sleep.

Does this make you feel better?

☐ **Not really**   ☐ **A little better**   ☐ **A lot better**

4. Your friend gets steaming mad at your boyfriend or girlfriend and starts plotting how you can get even with him or her.

Does this make you feel better?

☐ **Not really**   ☐ **A little better**   ☐ **A lot better**

5. Your friend listens carefully—maybe even chokes back emotions—then says something like, "I'm so sorry this happened to you. I feel so sad that you are hurting. I know this relationship meant a lot to you. We'll hang in there with you."

Does this make you feel better?

☐ **Not really**   ☐ **A little better**   ☐ **A lot better**

Which response made you feel the best? Why?_____

_____

_____

_____

_____

The rest of Romans 12:15 reads, "If they are sad, share their sorrow."

Earlier you discovered that sharing in a friend's joy multiplies his or her joy. But sharing in a friend's sorrow has the opposite effect. It divides, or *decreases* your friend's sorrow. The formula might look like this:

Friend's Sorrow ÷ Your Sorrow = Less Sorrow for Friend

This is how comfort works. When you identify with the pain and hurt of a friend and share the sorrow, God miraculously reduces your friend's pain. *Comfort* means to "ease the grief or trouble of another."

A 911 friend is someone who affirms the joys of another and increases that person's happiness. A 911 friend is also someone who affirms the sorrow of another and decreases the hurt and pain.

Prayer

Ask God to help you be a 911 friend who both increases the joys and decreases the sorrows of others this week.

_____

_____

_____

_____

_____

_____

_____

_____

A *911* Friend Is Affirming

CHAD'S STORY CONTINUES

had and his father practically lived at the hospital over the weekend, going home late at night only to sleep, shower, and change clothes. Family members, neighbors, and church friends were helpful and supportive. Neighbors took over the care of the Rogerses' two big dogs during the day. Friends brought meals and flowers to the hospital. And a number of people visited at the hospital as father and son stayed in the ICU waiting room. Chad most appreciated the timely visits of Doug and Jenny Shaw.

Chad slept only a few fitful hours on Friday and Saturday nights. Awaking very early each morning, he prayed that the horrors of Friday afternoon were only a bad dream. He lay in bed for several anxious minutes, imagining that Mom, Dad, and Matty were waiting to eat breakfast with him in the kitchen. But when he found his dad alone in the kitchen each morning, huddled over a cup of coffee and weeping, cold reality broke over him again.

On Sunday morning, Ben and Chad attended their church's early service before driving to the hospital. Soon after they arrived, Chad's best friend, Rob, died. Chad left his mother's bedside long enough to grieve with Rob's parents, Doug and Jenny, and a group of kids from the youth group who had come to the hospital after church. Chad missed Rob terribly. He also confided to Doug that he felt a little responsible for Rob's death. "If I hadn't begged him to come with me Friday night, he wouldn't have been in the van." Doug's care and understanding really helped.

Sunday afternoon, with the help of Pastor O'Neill, Ben and Chad started talking about Matthew's funeral. But Ben decided to postpone the service until the doctors could give him a clearer prognosis for Margaret. Beth, Chad's older sister, refused to talk about the funeral. She spent a few hours at the hospital on Saturday, but she showed little emotion. She preferred to be with her friends in town as her father and brother waited and prayed for Margaret to show a faint sign of recovery.

Monday morning, after consulting with the neurosurgeon, Ben approached his son in the ICU waiting room, where he sat with Doug. Chad studied his father's face. It was shadowed with the grief they had both carried since Friday night.

Ben sat down beside his son and spoke softly with great sadness in his voice. "Chad, I have very sad news. Dr. Nordvall just told me that Mom is not going to come out of the coma. He consulted other brain specialists, and they agree. She is not going to make it. It's now only a matter of time."

Chad dropped his head as he choked back the tears. "I don't know what to say, Dad," he said at last.

"That's all right, son," Ben assured. "I'm going to find Beth and tell her the doctor's news. We can all get together later this morning."

After his dad left, Chad talked with Doug for a few minutes, and they shared a brief time of prayer. Doug left for work, promising that he would be back around noon to check up on him.

Discovery Day

3

Chad found himself alone in the room with his mother. He stared for several minutes at the still form on the bed as the respirator pumped life into his mother's body breath by breath. The large, dark bruises on her pasty white face were tinged with sickly yellow. Her eyelids were taped closed. The woman looked more like a stranger than like Chad's mom.

Leaning close to his mother's ear, Chad whispered, "What should I do, Mom? I don't want you to die. I miss you already." Realizing there would be no response, Chad bowed his head. "Lord, I need to know what to do. I want You to perform a miracle and heal my mother. But if You choose not to do it, let me know. I can't stand to see her this way." Feeling exhausted in every way, Chad leaned back in the chair and fell asleep.

Early that afternoon, the family, along with Pastor O'Neill, invited close friends to gather around Margaret for prayer. Chad, however, declined the invitation. He waited outside with some others, staying close to Doug. "This really isn't happening, Doug, not to me."

"I know. It's unreal, like a bad nightmare."

"Mom can't die now; she just can't. She has to be here when I graduate and go off to college. We have so many plans. She just can't die. It isn't fair."

"I'm so sorry you won't have your mother to share in all that, Chad," Doug consoled him. "What else have you been feeling?"

Chad hesitated. "Sometimes I feel mad. Is that wrong?"

Doug patted his friend's shoulder. "Anger is a common, normal reaction. Tell me about it."

"I'm mad at the other driver for letting the truck cross the centerline. And why doesn't the county have wider roads? Maybe Mom could have swerved around the truck." Chad paused to wipe a small tear from his eye. "And I'm a little mad at God for letting this happen. He could have kept that truck from crossing the line. Why didn't He? The truck could have hit someone else's car, someone who didn't have any children."

Doug nodded. "It's hard to understand why it happened this way, isn't it?" He paused for a few seconds and then continued, "Anything else going on inside that you want to talk about?"

Chad looked away for a moment. Then he answered in a voice he hoped would not carry beyond them. "I think what happened to Mom and Matty may be partly my fault."

"Your fault? What do you mean?"

Chad dropped his head. "I haven't been very consistent in my devotions lately. If I had been praying for my family like I should, maybe Mom wouldn't have been in the crash."

"Oh, Chad," Doug said, "I'm so sorry that you've been bothered by such a thought."

Chad went on. "Last night I confessed it to God. I told Him that I would be more faithful and obedient to Him if He would just let Mom live." At that moment, Ben and Pastor O'Neill pushed through the door and slowly entered the room. Chad looked up, sensing the news in his father's face. "But I guess my prayer was too late."

There were only a few tears as Ben reported to those assembled in the room, "Margaret has gone to be with the Lord—and with Matthew." As family members and close friends embraced each other and left the hospital in twos and threes, they seemed relieved and grateful that Margaret's brief suffering was over. But her fifteen-year-old son was still struggling with a storm of conflicting feelings.

Before leaving the hospital, Doug took Chad aside for one last comment. "None of this is your fault, Chad," he whispered with compassion in his gaze. "But don't worry. I'll be here to help you get through it."

Your 911 Response

A lot of people tried to comfort Chad in the hospital. They all meant well, but not everything they said or did eased Chad's pain. Sometimes we confuse a word of advice, a pep talk, or an attempt to explain the painful circumstance as comfort. But whether your friend needs comfort for a deep sorrow or just a minor hurt, remember that real comfort involves identifying with that person's pain and sharing in his or her sorrow.

What Comfort Is Not

Some of Chad's experiences in the hospital are good examples of what comfort is *not.* Put a "C" in front of each statement that you think reflects comfort and an "X" in front of each statement that you think does not.

1. _____ "God must need your little brother in heaven more than we do."

2. _____ "I know it hurt a lot, and we really hurt with you."

3. _____ "At least Matthew didn't suffer long."

4. _____ "It hurts me to see you hurt so—I'm so sorry."

5. _____ "You should be thankful that God let you have Matty for six years."

Did you put an "X" on 1, 3, and 5? Those statements don't really provide much comfort. They may be true and are meant to help, but it does not reflect someone identifying with the hurt and then sharing in that hurt. Let's take a look at what some people might call comfort but really isn't comfort.

Comfort Is Not Problem Solving

"In my opinion, the reason this happened to you is . . . "

• There is a time for problem solving, but does knowing the cause of a hurt help *you* when you need a friend to share in your pain?   ❑ **Yes**   ❑ **No**

Comfort Is Not a Teaching Session

"In these kinds of situations, God instructs us to . . . "

• There is a time for teaching, but does knowing what to do next really help *you* if you need a friend to identify with your hurt?   ❑ **Yes**   ❑ **No**

Comfort Is Not a Pep Talk

"Come on, cheer up! The sun will come out tomorrow."

• There is a time for pep talks, but does "Put on a happy face" help *you* if you need a friend to share some of your sorrow?   ❑ **Yes**   ❑ **No**

Comfort Is Not Advice

"If I were you, the next time this happens, I would . . . "

• There is a time for good counsel, but does a word of advice help *you* if you need a friend to share in your grief?   ❑ **Yes**   ❑ **No**

When your friends are hurting, they may eventually need problem solving, teaching, pep talks, and advice. But they need comfort first. God's Word is full of examples of comfort. And Jesus is our star example.

How Did Jesus Respond When His Friends Were Hurting?

News flash! Ancient newspapers (discovered by archaeologists from Eastern Bogus University) report conflicting accounts of Jesus arriving too late for Lazarus's funeral. Compare these two accounts.

JESUS COME LATELY

BETHANY— Area businessman, Lazarus, died this week. His allegedly close friend, Jesus, a rabbi from Nazareth, showed up four days late for the funeral. Lazarus is survived by two sisters, Mary and Martha. Sources close to the sisters report that this rabbi was a miracle worker who could have kept the man from dying, but pressing teaching duties in Judea delayed his arrival. One man close to the family was quoted as saying, "I have never known such a hardhearted rabbi. He called himself a friend of the family, but he didn't lift a finger to help. When he finally arrived, all he did was teach us hard-to-understand lessons."

Area residents agree that the rabbi's actions dim his chances of being elected Messiah, if he ever decides to run.

THE COMFORTING RABBI

BETHANY— Popular teacher, Jesus of Nazareth, arrived in Bethany yesterday four days after his close friend, Lazarus, died. While some local citizens were critical of the rabbi for not preventing the man's death, others were impressed by the way he responded to the surviving sisters, Mary and Martha.

Eyewitnesses report that the great teacher had an extensive conversation with Martha. But when he saw her sister, Mary, weeping, something extraordinary happened.

"Jesus stood there for a moment watching his dear friend cry," one witness remarked. "You could see that he was deeply moved by her sorrow, almost visibly shaken. Then tears began to flow down his cheeks. I'm telling you, he really cried. He identified with that family's sorrow in a manner I have never seen before. We were all moved by it."

Read John 11:33–35 (NASB) below:

"When Jesus therefore saw [Mary] weeping, and the Jews who came with her, also weeping, He was deeply moved in spirit, and was troubled, and said, 'Where have you laid him?' They said to Him, 'Lord, come and see.' Jesus wept."

Which "newspaper report" was more accurate?

❑ "Jesus Come Lately"   ❑ "The Comforting Rabbi"

Do you know what happened shortly after Jesus cried? Jesus performed a major miracle: He raised Lazarus from the dead! So why was He crying if He knew Lazarus would soon be alive again?'

Think about it. Jesus knew He was going to raise Lazarus from the dead in a matter of minutes. Yet He wept in response to the grief of Mary and Martha. So what was He crying about? Was He crying for joy, knowing He would soon be reunited with His friend Lazarus? Was He crying to impress the crowd with His compassion? Whom do you think Christ's tears were for: for Himself or for Mary and Martha?

_____

_____

_____

_____

Comfort shares in the sorrows of others. Jesus knew how to comfort people who were hurting.

Prayer

Close by thanking God for Jesus, your comforting friend. Then tell God that you want to be a comforting friend to those around you this week.

_____

_____

_____

_____

_____

A 911 Friend Is Affirming

CHAD'S STORY CONTINUES

Discovery Day

The memorial service for Margaret and Matthew Rogers was scheduled for Friday morning at the church. At his father's encouragement, Chad decided to stay home from school for the week. It gave him time to grieve with Dad and Beth and other relatives, many of whom were visiting from out of state.

Chad was amazed at the practical support supplied by friends and church members like Doug and Jenny Shaw. He had expressed concern to Doug that he might fall behind on his schoolwork during his week away. So Doug went to the school, contacted each of Chad's teachers, and collected assignments Chad could do at home. Chad found it helpful to divert his concentration to homework a couple of hours each day.

Pastor O'Neill told Ben and Chad not to worry about fixing meals for themselves. Every evening, a different church family showed up at the house with a delicious covered-dish supper, plenty of food for the Rogerses and Chad's uncle and his family, who were staying with them for the week. Church families and friends in town volunteered to house other visiting relatives. And there was always someone available to run errands and help with household chores. Doug and Jenny Shaw were right in the middle of making sure Chad and his family were cared for in practical ways.

In addition to the support, Chad felt overwhelmed at the encouragement people shared with him and his family. Several bouquets and potted plants were delivered to the house every day. Scores of cards and letters arriving by mail were filled with kind words of concern and love. Many people called to share their love and sympathy and to ask how the family was doing. Chad was especially impressed by the oversized card the members of the church youth group sent to him. Everyone had written in it, signed it, and included a Scripture verse.

Even with all the support and encouragement, Chad had his down times. "I really get emotional around bedtime," he confided in Doug on Thursday evening. "Mom usually came in to chat and pray with me before I turned out the light. I miss that so much already." Chad and Doug were sipping blended fruit smoothies at the local health-food shop. Doug had invited him out just to ask how he was doing. Chad realized it felt good to be out of the house for a little while.

"I'm so sorry that you won't have that nightly visit with your Mom, Chad," Doug consoled.

Chad sipped his drink and continued, "I seem to cycle through those different feelings you talked to me about. Mostly I'm either very sad or very mad."

"That's OK, Chad," Doug said. "It's part of the grieving process."

"I'm worried about Beth though," Chad said with a little frown. "She hasn't cried once, and she doesn't want to talk about what happened to Mom or Matty. She spends most of the day with her friends or in her room alone. Is there anything I can do for her?"

"Two things come to mind," Doug answered. "First, comfort her as best you can. Think of the special times she enjoyed with your mother and—"

"Beth and Mom kept in touch on the computer," Chad interrupted. "They exchanged e-mail several times a week."

"OK, maybe you could say to her, 'Beth, I feel sorry that you won't be able to chat with Mom by e-mail anymore. I know that was very special to you.'"

"Just like you comforted me about missing my nightly visits with Mom."

"Exactly," Doug said with a wink. " And if you think of other areas where she is hurting about the loss of your mother and brother, you can offer words of comfort there too."

"I can do that," Chad assured, "because I'm sure Beth and I are struggling with some of the same areas about Mom and Matty."

"The second thing you can do is pray for her," Doug said. "Ask God to help her receive the comfort she needs. That's what Jenny and I have been praying for. And we're praying for you too, Chad, every day."

Chad poked at the frothy drink with his straw. "Thanks," he said meekly. "It means a lot that you check up on me. And thanks for the nice card you and Jenny sent. Dad and I have been real close this week, but it's great to know that you and Jenny are here too."

Doug nodded. "That's what it's all about to be in a family of believers, isn't it?" Chad smiled and agreed.

Chad woke up the next morning dreading the funeral, expecting it to be sad and depressing. But he was wrong. There were many tears in the crowded sanctuary, especially in the rows where Chad sat with his family. But Pastor O'Neill used the service to praise God for the lives of Chad's mother and brother. The songs sung and words spoken assured Chad that God is good and gracious when tragedy strikes. Even the brief service of committal at the cemetery had an uplifting note as Pastor O'Neill reminded the family of the resurrection to come at Christ's Second Coming.

Your 911 Response

Doug and others are identifying with Chad's feelings of loss. As they express their sorrow to him, it eases his grief. That's what comfort does. You may not be called upon that often to comfort a friend who has lost a loved one. But almost every day, people around you are hurting from some kind of loss, disappointment, or discouragement. And they are just as much in need of comfort as someone like Chad.

With so many people around you in need of your comfort, you may expect to run dry emotionally. Sharing in the sorrows of so many hurting people could be depressing, right? Really, it's not! Comforting others is actually a high!

Comforting Others Is a High?

"Get serious!" you say. "Comforting others cannot be a high. It has to be draining to keep giving and giving and giving."

Let's do the math. For example, let's say you have a 100-milligram capacity for comfort. But Friend A needs 75 milligrams of comfort due to a relational breakup. If you shared what your friend needs, how much comfort would you have left?

Your 100 mg. of comfort

Friend A - 75 mg. for broken relationship

_____ mg. of remaining comfort

Now Friend B comes along. He needs 50 milligrams of comfort because his team lost a big game. Losing a game usually doesn't hurt as badly as losing a friend, but it still hurts. So Friend B needs 50 milligrams of comfort. If you comfort Friend A and Friend B, how much comfort will you have left?

> Your 100 mg. of comfort
>
> Friend A - 75 mg. for broken relationship
>
> Friend B - 50 mg. for big bad loss
>
> _____ mg. of remaining comfort

Conclusion: *I don't have enough comfort to go around. I must give out my comfort in small doses or I will totally run out.*

Do you agree with the above conclusion?

❏ **Agree**   ❏ **Disagree**

Your Source of Comfort

If you agreed with that conclusion, you are right. If all you have to give is the comfort you have, you will run dry in a hurry. The principle we have discussed earlier in this course applies here: You can't give what you don't have. And you can't meet the need for comfort in all your hurting friends if you are your own source of comfort. You must tap into another source of comfort. You must learn to give out of God's supply.

Read the following scripture.

> "All praise to the God and Father of our Lord Jesus Christ. He is the source of every mercy and the God who comforts us. He comforts us in all our troubles so that we can comfort others. When others are troubled, we will be able to give them the same comfort God has given us" (2 Cor. 1:3–4).

1. Who is the source of mercy and comfort? _____

2. What is one reason God comforts us? _____

_____

3. When others are troubled, whose comfort do we give them? _____

Do you see why comforting others can be a high? God has an endless supply of comfort, because He is the God of all comfort. His comfort will never run out. When your friends need comfort, you can supply that need from your abundant source. God will empower you with a miraculous and rewarding ministry of comfort to your friends. God is actually there to ease the pain and share His healing through you. That's a spiritual and emotional high!

Receive in Order to Give

In order to give comfort, you must receive comfort. But how do you receive the comfort you need to share with others?

God comforts us so we can comfort _____.

God gives us His comfort through _____.

"You can be sure that the more we suffer for Christ, the more God will shower us with his comfort through Christ" (2 Cor.1:5).

Do you see it? God delivers His comfort to you: ✔ through Christ
                                                  ✔ through others

God is the source of all true comfort, and He is pleased to channel some of His healing comfort through your friends to you. Of course, He will also provide it directly from Christ to you.

Comfort through Christ

We have discovered that God wants us to comfort others by identifying with their troubles and sharing in their pain. But how does Christ comfort us? Check (✔) the boxes that you think apply.

❑   Christ says to sing our troubles away.
❑   Christ gives us the power to forget our troubles and pain.
❑   Christ has suffered like we have and he shares in our pain.
❑   Christ helps us never to feel any pain or suffering.

Read the following thoughtfully:

"Since [Christ] himself has gone through suffering and temptation, he is able to help us when we are being tempted. . . . This High Priest of ours understands our weaknesses, for he faced all of the same temptations we do, yet he did not sin. So let us come boldly to the throne of our gracious God. There we will receive his mercy, and we will find grace to help us when we need it" (Heb. 2:18; 4:15–16).

The Bible says that Christ has also gone through suffering and temptation and that we can receive His mercy and grace to help us. But has Christ really suffered like you and your friends have suffered? Check (✔) any circumstances or feelings below that both you and Christ have experienced:

❑   I have felt **rejected** (Christ was rejected by His own people.)
❑   I have felt **abandoned** (Christ was abandoned by His own disciples.)
❑   I have felt **misunderstood** (Christ was misunderstood by His followers.)
❑   I have been **ridiculed** (Christ was mocked and ridiculed at His trial.)
❑   I have been **betrayed** (Christ was betrayed by Judas.)
❑   I have been **criticized** (Christ was criticized by the Pharisees.)
❑   I have felt **neglected** (Christ was neglected by His disciples, who slept instead of praying with Him in the Garden of Gethsemane.)
❑   I have **suffered the death of a loved one** (Christ suffered the loss of Lazarus.)
❑   I have **suffered the loss of a friend** (Christ suffered the denial of Peter.)
❑   I have **suffered physical pain** (Christ suffered a beating and the horrible death of crucifixion.)

Christ is God, and He can identify with anything you have gone through or are going through or will ever go through. He is the God of all comfort, and He encourages you to come boldly to Him to receive His comfort and help.

Confirm Your Time with Your Friendship Partner

God is also pleased to share some of His comfort through you to your friends. Tomorrow's Discovery Day Five is an exercise for you and your friendship partner to experience together. Contact your partner and confirm the time and place to go over Discovery Day Five together.

Prayer

Close by thanking God that He comforts you through Christ. Tell Him how you feel that He identifies with your pain and hurt and is with you during troubled times. Thank Him that He affirms you in the good times and identifies with you when you feel joy.

_____

_____

_____

_____

_____

_____

_____

A **911** Friend Is Affirming

CHAD'S STORY CONTINUES

Doug picked up Chad at 9:30 Saturday morning. They had not had a day out at the driving range since before Chad's mom and brother died three months earlier. Doug had been away at a business conference all week, so the first thing he asked as they drove away was, "How are you doing, Chad?"

Chad knew Doug would ask, because he usually did. "I'm doing pretty OK. I still miss Mom a lot, and I have my emotional moments, but I know it's part of the process. I'm so glad you told me about the different stages of grief. If I didn't know they were part of the process, I might think there was something wrong with me for feeling angry or trying to bargain with God at times."

Chad shared a little more about his week, then Doug asked. "How about Beth? Is she doing all right?"

Chad sighed. "It's hard to tell, because she is away at school. She calls about once a week, but she doesn't talk about Mom or Matty or the accident. I have been praying for her, and I've tried to comfort her like you suggested. But I think she is still hurting and doesn't know how to deal with it."

Doug nodded. "Some people have a difficult time dealing with their pain and receiving comfort. Just keep praying for her and looking for ways to share comfort. Jenny and I will do the same."

"Thanks."

Doug turned onto the main highway lead-

ing to the driving range then asked, "What has been the greatest help to you in getting through your times of denial, anger, and depression this month?"

Chad thought for a moment. "Well, one thing is that I have hope. I know that I will see Mom and Matty and Rob again in heaven someday. I have heard the Bible verses about heaven since I was a small child, but in the last few weeks that truth has really become real to me. I don't know how people make it without the hope of being with Christ and seeing their loved ones again.

"And I guess another thing that's been helpful is that there are people like you to be with. My close friends at church have been great about spending time with me when I'm missing Rob. And if I need to talk, some of them talk it out with me, just like you do. It has brought us all closer together."

"That's what happens when friends really comfort one another like the Bible says," Doug interjected.

"And Dad has been great. Some days he will sit down with me and ask what I'm thinking. At other times, we don't even have to talk. We just hug, and sometimes we even cry. I don't know how, but being together and opening up to each other seems to ease the pain of losing Mom and Matty. We are closer than we've ever been."

"That's great, Chad."

"And do you know what? Sometimes I am able to think about Mom and Matty and Rob and enjoy the good memories without the pain getting in the way. I still miss them a lot, but I am also very thankful for the time I had with each of them. I'm sure that the hope I

Discovery Day

5

WEEK THREE

69

feel and the comfort of others—plus time—will eventually heal even my deepest hurts."

"I'm happy to hear that for at least two reasons," Doug said. "One, I'm just happy for how God is helping you through this very difficult time. Two, I want to talk to you about Marty Keller."

"Marty Keller? He's the new freshman in our youth group, right?"

"Right," Doug said. "Marty and his family started attending our church about a month ago."

Chad shrugged. "I don't really know him very well yet."

"Neither do I," Doug said. "But Pastor O'Neill called this morning to tell us that Marty's grandfather died suddenly of a stroke yesterday. Marty was very close to his grandfather, and he is really hurting."

"Really?" Chad asked. "I'll bet Marty could use some comfort right now."

"That's what I thought," Doug agreed. Then he was silent.

It didn't take Chad long to take the hint. He turned to Doug and smiled. "Maybe we could stop by Marty's house on the way to the driving range—just for a couple of minutes. I guess I have some comfort I could share with him."

"Just what I was thinking. Let's go on a mission of comfort," Doug said as he turned the car in the direction of the Keller home.

Your Friendship 911 Exercise

God's comfort works! Comfort simply means allowing God to help you identify with the pain or loss or grief of a friend, then God does the rest.

Walk through this exercise with your friendship partner. Simply follow the directions and experience the increasing of each other's joy and the decreasing of each other's troubles.

Affirm a Joy

Start with increasing each other's joy.

1. Think of something positive that happened this week, something that made you happy. Each of you write down what happened and how it made you feel.

_____

_____

_____

_____

2. Take turns sharing your experiences. Don't get into a long discussion about the event or situation that caused the joy. Just increase your friend's joy by being excited and happy with him or her.

When your friend identified with your positive experience and shared in your joy, how did it make you feel? Share your answer with your friend.

Affirm a Hurt

1. Think of something that recently caused you disappointment or discouragement, perhaps an incident that resulted in some personal pain. Each of you write down the situation and how it made you feel.

_____

_____

_____

2. Take turns sharing your painful or disappointing feelings without spending much time on the details of what happened. Focus more on how the incident affected you.

After your friendship partner shares the situation, be a channel of God's comfort to him or her.

Warning! Be Careful!

Don't give advice

"If I were you, I would . . . "

Don't give a pep talk

"Come on, cheer up."

Don't teach a lesson

"In these situations you should . . . "

Don't try to solve the problem

"I think this happened because . . . "

Do, however, identify with what your friend is feeling right now. Consider how God identifies with your friend. His tender heart feels your friend's pain. He longs to wrap His arms around your friend and say, "I'm so sorry you had to go through that. I hurt for you and want you to know I'm here to go through it with you."

Can you take those words and share them as your own? Will you join God in sharing His comfort? As you do, you will experience the miracle of God's comfort and the comfort of a 911 friend.

When your friend identified with your hurt or disappointment, how did it make you feel? Did you sense the ministry of comfort? Explain.

_____

_____

_____

_____

Consider using this time as a way to encourage your youth group. Agree to share with them what happened during this exercise. It will be an example of what a 911 friend looks like, and it will honor the God of all comfort. He is smiling on the two of you right now for honoring Him in His ministry of healing hurts by comforting one another.

Prayer

Close in a prayer of thanksgiving to your comforting God.

_____

_____

_____

_____

The PROJECT 911 Collection

The story of Chad in this week's workbook is adapted from the small book entitled *My Friend Is Struggling with the Death of a Loved One*. The book is designed as a giveaway book you can read and then give to a friend who has experienced the tragic loss of someone dear. Beyond the fictional story, this book provides practical steps for going through the grieving process and finding comfort during a painful loss.

If you want one or more of these books for a friend, contact your youth leader. He or she may have a number of copies on hand. If not, this and other books in this collection can be ordered in bulk by calling 1-800-933-9673 ext. 9-2039. Or you can purchase copies of this book at your local Christian bookstore.

WEEK FOUR

A 911 Friend Is Supportive

STEPHANIE'S STORY

Stephanie peeked through the venetian blinds, watching her mother's car drive away until it disappeared around the corner. She kept her eyes glued on the empty street in front of the house for several seconds to make sure the car didn't come back.

"Stephanie, you should see yourself," Kate said with a little laugh. "You look like some kind of spy." Stephanie Cooper and Kate Holmes, both seventeen, had been best friends since fourth grade. They met because their older brothers had been best friends in high school. Summer vacation was nearly over for the two girls. The senior year they had anticipated so long together started in two weeks.

"Mom sometimes forgets things and has to come back," Stephanie said, still watching the street. Her mother, a grocery checker, worked the late shift today—4:30 until midnight. Stephanie wanted to make sure her mom was gone for the evening, because she didn't want to be interrupted.

"Would you rather catch a movie first and go for pizza later?" Kate said. She was sitting cross-legged on the living room floor studying the entertainment section of the newspaper. "We can get into the theater for half-price before six."

Convinced that her mother was gone, Stephanie finally turned away from the window to face her friend. She released a long sigh. "I don't want to go out tonight."

Kate looked up from the paper, surprised. "You told me last night you wanted to do pizza and a movie tonight."

Stephanie sat down on the floor with her friend. "I know, but that was last night."

"Do you still have a touch of the flu?"

Stephanie dropped her head. "No, I don't have the flu."

"Well then . . . what?" Kate waited for an explanation.

Stephanie picked at her fingernails. "We have to talk," she said, avoiding eye contact.

Those four words were among the most serious spoken between the two friends. Both knew that the topic to follow was important. They had used the phrase only a few times during the nearly seven years they had been friends. Stephanie used it once because a cute boy had turned her close relationship with Kate into a fierce rivalry. After they talked, they decided no boy was worth jeopardizing their friendship. And when Kate said "We have to talk" during their sophomore year, it was to announce that she had trusted Christ as her Savior through the ministry of her youth group at church. Stephanie was so impressed with the change in her friend that she began attending church with her and trusted Christ two months later. As "sisters in Christ," their friendship had grown even stronger.

Stephanie felt Kate's eyes boring into the top of her head. "What's wrong, Steph?" she said, totally serious.

Stephanie didn't want to answer. She had spent nearly three months trying to convince herself that there was nothing wrong. Up until two hours ago, she almost believed it.

"What is it, Stephanie?" Kate probed with loving sisterly insistence. She leaned forward and touched her friend on the knee. "You know you have to tell me. Whatever it is, you know it's OK."

A tide of despair mixed with panic rolled up Stephanie's throat. When she finally looked up, her chin was trembling and tears flooded her eyes. "Kate, I'm pregnant." Then the dam burst, and Stephanie could say no more. Burying her face in her hands, she sobbed in anguish.

"Stephanie, no!" Kate shrieked in disbelief. She rolled up on her knees and gripped her friend by the shoulders. For a full minute, Stephanie cried hard, and Kate just held on to her and let her own tears flow.

As the crying subsided, Kate was in Stephanie's face. "What happened? Did you miss a period? Some girls miss periods, and they're not pregnant, Steph. Maybe it's something else. You can't be sure."

It was another half-minute before Stephanie could respond. Wiping her eyes and nose with tissues Kate provided, she said, "I'm sure. I went to the doctor today, a clinic across town. I already missed two periods. The flu I told you about—that I told myself was the flu—was morning sickness. I'm almost three months pregnant, Kate. I . . . I . . . " Another wave of tears choked off her words.

"Oh, Stephanie," Kate whimpered, tearing up herself. She enveloped Stephanie in her arms and cried with her, repeating softly, "It's OK, I'm here. We'll get through this together."

After a couple of minutes, they were again facing each other, seated on the floor. Kate continued to hold Stephanie's hand. "What about your mom?" Kate said, dabbing her eyes.

Stephanie slowly shook her head. "She doesn't know. Nobody knows except me and you—and the doctor at the clinic."

Another minute passed in silence, except for an occasional sniffle. Stephanie drank in the comfort of her friend being here for her. She appreciated the fact that Kate was not bugging her with the inevitable questions: who, when, and how? But she realized that Kate deserved to know the answers.

Your 911 Response

Stephanie's life is about to change—drastically. She's pregnant, and she will face many complications and burdens in the months ahead. But her friend Kate said, "We'll get through this together." What did she mean by that? Kate meant she would be an **available**, caring, listening and safe friend. She meant she would be an **accepting**, forgiving, nonjudgmental friend who loved Stephanie regardless of what she had done. It also meant that Kate would be a **comforting** friend, one who shares in the pain to relieve the hurt. Stephanie needs a friend right now to be all of that. But she needs something else from her friend: Stephanie needs Kate's **support**.

You don't find friends facing problems as big as Stephanie's every week. But you do have friends, both guys and girls, who can use your support practically every week of the month. Does supporting your friends mean becoming their "grunt," doing anything and everything your friends want or need you to do? Or does it just mean you are there for them in spirit, supporting your friends emotionally? What does it really mean to be a supportive 911 friend?

Support Does As Support Is

Imagine that your friend Cal asks you to go to the mall with him after school. You say, "OK, but I promised the coach I would move some benches in the gym first." Cal says, "Fine. I'll go and help out." When you arrive at the gym, he parks himself in a chair with his hand-held video game while you do your chore. You wonder what he meant when he said he would "help out."

You are supposed to move several benches out of the storage room to the gym floor. But the benches are eight feet long, and the doorway to the storage room is rather narrow. "Lift the front end up higher," Cal calls out as he watches you struggle to get the first bench through the doorway. "Now turn the bench on its side . . . no, the other way. Now swing the legs out the doorway first." You swing the bench one way and then the other, banging against the wall. Then a corner of the bench cracks into the door molding, leaving a big dent. You still haven't moved one bench out of the storage room.

"No, back up again," Cal instructs from his perch on the chair. "Now pick up the back end and move it to the left. . . . OK, now pick up the front end and slide it around." You catch your finger between the bench and the doorjamb and yelp. The pain causes you to drop the bench, which lands on your foot, and you yelp in pain again. You can't believe how *un*helpful your "helpful" friend is.

Cal looks up from his video game. "C'mon, hurry up," he barks. "Move those benches so we can get going." You limp out of the storage room, holding your throbbing finger.

Check (✔) the statement below that best represents what you might say to Cal:

- ❏ "Will you go find me a Band-Aid and a power drink please?"
- ❏ "This is taking longer than I thought. I'll meet you at the mall later."
- ❏ "You sure are good at video games."
- ❏ "Where did you learn so much about moving benches?"
- ❏ "Will you please stop *telling me* what to do and come over here and *help me!*"

Cal wasn't very helpful. He may have thought he was being supportive by barking out instructions, but you really didn't need that kind of support.

How would you define the support you needed? _____

_____

_____

Jesus said, "And I will ask the Father, and He will give you another Helper, that He may be with you forever;" (John 14:16 NASB).

The Helper, of course, is the Holy Spirit. The word Jesus used for *Helper* means "one called alongside" to help. It's like someone coming alongside to lift the load or share the weight of a burden or struggle. That's what **support** means—**coming alongside to lift up a friend in need.**

"Carry each other's burdens, and in this way you will fulfill the law of Christ" (Gal. 6:2 NIV).

Were you aware that being a supportive friend is actually part of obeying Christ?
❏ Yes   ❏ No   ❏ Wasn't sure

Another translation of Galatians 6:2 says, "Share each other's troubles and problems, and in this way obey the law of Christ."

Check (✔) the circumstances below that might fall into the category of troubles, problems, or burdens your friends have had in the past or have now.

1. Is sick and behind on schoolwork.
2. Stole top government secrets and is hiding out in Cuba.
3. Is depressed over a broken relationship, a failing grade, a conflict with someone, _____, etc.
4. Is suffering from a physical injury or disability.
5. Is five million dollars in debt from a weekend trip to Las Vegas.
6. Is struggling to determine God's will about attending college, choosing a career, summer activities, etc.

✳ Might a friend in one of these circumstances need your *emotional or relational* support?
   ❏ **Yes**   ❏ **No**   ❏ **Don't know**
✳ Might a friend in one of these circumstances need your *physical or academic* support?
   ❏ **Yes**   ❏ **No**   ❏ **Don't know**
✳ Might a friend in one of these circumstances need your *spiritual* support?
   ❏ **Yes**   ❏ **No**   ❏ **Don't know**

Your friends may need you to come alongside them with some form of supportive help in all the above circumstances. But carrying burdens means more than *doing* supportive things. It also means *being* supportive. Friendship 911 support *does* in actions what support *is* in attitudes.

Prayer

Close this time in prayer by asking God to come alongside you right now and help you be the supportive 911 friend He wants you to be. Ask Him to help you see how you can both *be* and *do* support this week to a friend.

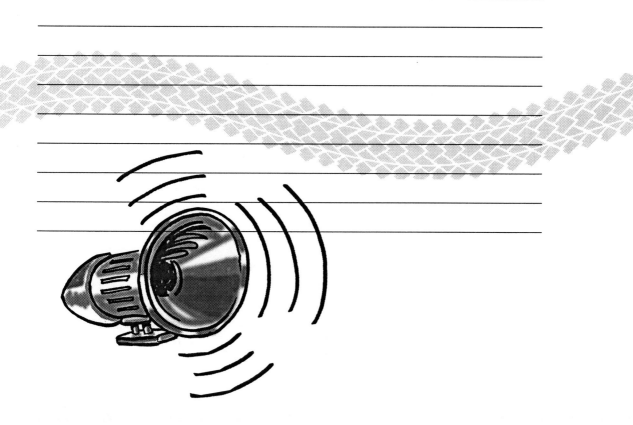

Stephanie spoke softly. "Remember when Mom and I flew to the West Coast for my grandmother's funeral the first of June?"

"Yes. You were gone a whole week."

Stephanie nodded. "Well, there's this guy back there—Brent. As a kid, I saw him every summer when we went to my dad's parents' house for vacation. We played together and had crushes on each other—just kids' stuff, that's all. After Dad and Mom divorced four years ago, I stopped going back there in the summer. I never thought about Brent again.

"Seeing him in June, I couldn't believe it. He was so different, so grown up. When I wasn't with my family, I was with Brent. We had so much fun, and by the end of the week I was spending most of my time with him. The old childish attraction came back, except we weren't kids anymore. One thing led to another, and on Friday night we . . . didn't stop.

"The whole week was unreal, like being in a movie or something. I kept telling myself that what I did back there didn't count. I came back home wishing I hadn't done it and trying to brush the whole thing out of my mind. I didn't tell you anything because I guess I didn't want to admit there was anything to tell. Then I missed a period and started feeling sick in the morning. When I missed my second period, I knew I had to find out for sure. I put it off until today. I might have been able to keep denying it, except the test proves I'm pregnant."

The girls were silent for several seconds. Finally, Kate said, "Do you think you should tell Brent?"

Stephanie looked away, misty-eyed. "I don't know what to think, Kate," she said, sighing heavily. "My whole life changed two hours ago. I'm so embarrassed and ashamed. I feel so dirty. All the plans we had for our senior year . . . " Her words trailed off to a sad whimper. "I don't know what to do."

Kate straightened up. "I know somebody who can help. We need to go see Jenny." Jenny Shaw had discipled each girl individually for several weeks after they trusted Christ.

"I can't tell Jenny about this," Stephanie objected. "I can hardly bear the thought of telling my mom. I don't want anybody at church to know. I just want to . . . go away."

Kate's face registered shock. "You don't mean to the West Coast, do you?"

Stephanie felt lost. After several seconds she said, "I don't know, Kate. I'm not in love with Brent, but maybe someday I could be. I don't know what to do about telling my mom. And I don't know what to do about this baby. I just want to run away and hide."

"I love you, Stephanie, and I can't let you do that," Kate said firmly. "We will get through this like we get through everything else: together. But we can't do it alone. We have to call Jenny. She'll know what to do, and she won't blab to anyone."

Stephanie knew her friend was right, but she felt so embarrassed. "Maybe Jenny won't have time to talk to us," she argued feebly.

It was all the permission Kate needed. Reaching for the phone book, she said, "We won't know until we ask." Kate looked up the

Discovery Day

number of Doug's and Jenny's quick-print shop and tapped it into the phone.

"Kate, I—"

"Trust me, Steph," Kate interrupted. "I won't do anything to embarrass you." Then Jenny Shaw came on the line. As Stephanie listened, Kate arranged for the three of them to get together tonight. Jenny's husband, Doug, was leaving for the church men's retreat at 6:00. Kate and Stephanie would pick up a pizza and take it to Jenny's house by 6:30 for an evening of "girl talk" and a sleepover. Kate mentioned nothing about the shocking news.

Two hours later, Stephanie reluctantly followed Kate up to Jenny's door. She and Kate were loaded down with bedrolls, overnight bags, and a large five-topping boxed pizza. Jenny's cheery welcome and sisterly hug boosted Stephanie's spirits. "I'm so glad you called," Jenny said. "With Doug gone for the weekend, I needed company tonight."

Stephanie tried to hide the dark tide of despair that had been rising steadily inside her since the clinic visit. But as they sat down around the pizza box, Jenny eyed the sad face across the table and asked, "Is everything OK?" Stephanie lost it again. During a torrent of tears, Stephanie's story of pregnancy tumbled out while the pizza got cold in the box. Jenny and Kate moved in beside Stephanie. "It's OK, Stephanie," they said, crying with her. "Let it all out." The hesitance Stephanie had felt about telling Jenny quickly melted in the warmth of her comforting embrace and sympathetic tears.

"My life is ruined," Stephanie moaned sadly. "I don't know if I can finish high school, let alone get through college."

"I know it hurts a lot right now," Jenny consoled her. "I'm so sorry."

"And I'm so ashamed. How can I face my friends at school? And how can I tell them I'm a Christian after what I've done?"

Jenny rubbed her back gently. "I so sorry, Stephanie. But Kate and I are here for you."

"Worst of all, I have committed a terrible sin," Stephanie said in quavering voice. "Premarital sex is against the Bible. It's something I promised God I would never do. I know He is disappointed with me. And Kate and I committed that we would both be virgins when we married. I failed God and my best friend. I feel so worthless."

After a few minutes, Jenny suggested that they spend some time praying together. She encouraged Stephanie to bring her feelings and guilt to God while she and Kate prayed with her silently.

As they all held hands, Stephanie prayed, "God, You know what I'm feeling before I even tell You, but I need to say that I'm feeling so ashamed right now. I wish I could turn back the clock and change what I did. But I can't. I also wish these awful feelings would go away, but I can't stop feeling them."

Jenny prayed next. "Dear Lord, I hurt for Stephanie right now. There's no way I can really know what she's going through, but it hurts to see her feeling so terrible about herself. You can look into her heart and see the pain. Help her to know that You haven't stopped loving her, that You are willing to carry her sorrow and ease her pain."

Kate added a prayer for God to comfort her friend. Then Stephanie prayed again. "God, I have sinned. I realize that I have disobeyed You and hurt You. My pregnancy is a result of my disobedience. It's hard to accept, but I also know that You love me. You sent Your Son to die for my sins. So I ask You to forgive me right now and take control of my life from this moment on."

Your 911 Response

Stephanie is fortunate to have supportive friends like Kate and Jenny—two friends who are willing to come alongside her to lift her up. That's the kind of friend you need sometimes, right? And those around you occasionally need your support too. But what does it take to be a supportive 911 friend? It's all about *doing* supportive things that flow out of your *being* a supportive friend.

Being a Supportive Friend

You are struggling under a heavy load. You need help studying for a big exam or you need a friend to go with you to resolve a conflict or you just need someone to hang with because you're feeling a little low right now. What kind of a response are you looking for from a friend? Probably not any of these listed below. See if you can match each unsupportive response on the left with a poor attitude on the right (see the completed example).

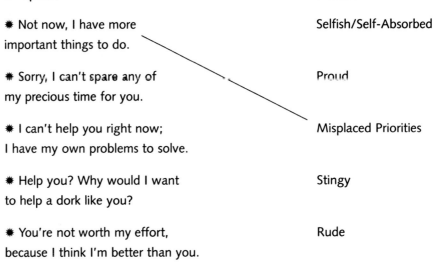

Response	Attitude
✳ Not now, I have more important things to do.	Selfish/Self-Absorbed
✳ Sorry, I can't spare any of my precious time for you.	Proud
✳ I can't help you right now; I have my own problems to solve.	Misplaced Priorities
✳ Help you? Why would I want to help a dork like you?	Stingy
✳ You're not worth my effort, because I think I'm better than you.	Rude

Real friends would not likely respond so bluntly and unkindly, and neither would you. Yet we all tend to be a little self-centered unless we continually cultivate an "others-focused" attitude. Following are Christlike attitudes we all need to develop to be a 911 friend.

Be Caring and Not Self-Absorbed

"If you think you are too important to help someone in need, you are only fooling yourself. You are really a nobody" (Gal. 6:3).

Being a supportive friend means having a caring attitude. What does Galatians 6:3 teach us? Check (✔) two statements that reflect this verse.

❑ When you think you are too important, you are actually a nobody.

❑ You are fooling yourself when you forget where you put your homework.

❑ People who think they are too important to help others are self-absorbed.

❑ A nobody is a person who is badly out of shape physically.

Be Humble and Unselfish

"Don't be selfish; don't live to make a good impression on others. Be humble, thinking of others as better than yourself. Don't think only about your own affairs, but be interested in others, too, and what they are doing" (Phil. 2:3–4).

Being a supportive friend means you have an unselfish and humble attitude. What would Philippians 2:3–4 look like in your life? Check (✔) two statements below that reflect these verses.

❑ If I smile a lot and do stuff for people, maybe I'll be really popular.

❑ I wonder how it's going with my friend Sean. There may be a way I can help him right now. I'll call him.

❑ Some kids are really putting Kristen down because she's not as smart as they are. I want to let her know that I admire her and that I'm her good friend.

❑ You really have to look out for yourself because no one else will, that's for sure!

Be Generous and Giving

"Give, and it will be given to you; good measure, pressed down, shaken together, running over, they will pour into your lap. For by your standard of measure it will be measured to you in return" (Luke 6:38 NASB).

Being a supportive friend means having a generous and giving attitude. Are there benefits to having a giving attitude? Check (✔) two statements below that reflect this verse.

❑ It doesn't pay to be generous because people will take advantage of your time and money.

❑ Before you give of your time or effort, always get the person to promise that he or she will give back to you.

❑ An unselfish giver eventually gets good things in return.

❑ The more you give to others, the more you will receive from others.

Improvement Necessary?

Does your attitude as a supportive friend need to improve? Check (✔) the response in each category that applies.

A Caring Attitude. How much more of a caring attitude do I need?

❑ a little more   ❑ a good amount more   ❑ a whole lot more

Prayer: Ask God to help you be less self-absorbed and more caring toward your friends.

_____

_____

_____

An Unselfish Attitude. How much more of an unselfish, humble attitude do I need?

❏ **a little more**   ❏ **a good amount more**   ❏ **a whole lot more**

Prayer: Ask God to help you be more unselfish with your time and energy toward your friends.

_____

_____

_____

A Giving Attitude. How much more of a giving attitude do I need?

❏ **a little more**   ❏ **a good amount more**   ❏ **a whole lot more**

Prayer: Ask God to help you to be more generous toward your friends.

_____

_____

_____

Schedule Time with Your Friendship Partner

Contact your partner today or tomorrow and confirm your time to meet to go over Discovery Day Five together.

We will meet on _____ (day); at _____(time); at

_____(place)

fter several more minutes of prayer and comforting words, Jenny said, "You know you have some decisions to make, Stephanie." Stephanie nodded. "But I don't think tonight is the best time. We're all pretty emotionally drained. I suggest that we eat dinner, watch a video or two, and just be together. Tomorrow morning after breakfast, we can start talking about these decisions. Would that be OK with both of you?"

Stephanie agreed quickly. "My brain is frazzled. I can't even think straight. Tomorrow would be much better." Kate nodded.

Then Stephanie said, "I just want to say that you two are incredible. Your support means so much to me and to have you here with me right now. I don't know what I would do without you."

"We love you, Steph," Kate said. "That's what friends are for."

After another round of caring embraces, Jenny said, "Now let's nuke this pizza and see how fast we can make it disappear!"

Stephanie slept better than she had expected. She woke up only a couple of times in the night after bad dreams. But she went right back to sleep both times. Just being with Kate and Jenny and allowing them to share in her pain seemed to lift some of the weight from her.

After a breakfast of homemade waffles and fruit, Jenny, Stephanie, and Kate moved into the family room with cups of hot tea. It was a conversation Stephanie wished she could avoid.

"It's very important that you tell your mother about your pregnancy right away, Stephanie," Jenny began.

Stephanie winced. "I know, but she will be so disappointed. It's been so hard on her since Dad left."

"Would you like me to go with you when you tell her?" Jenny said.

Stephanie released a sigh of relief. "I was hoping you would. Thanks."

"Is your mom home today? Can we talk to her later?" Jenny pressed.

"Yes, she's off today," Stephanie said, fidgeting nervously. "We can tell her today, I guess. But what do I say?"

"We'll talk about that soon," Jenny assured, "after you have a better idea what you're going to do. What about your father? I don't believe I know him."

Stephanie shook her head. "Dad left Mom four years ago. He lives out of state. We don't hear from him much. I also have an older brother at the university."

Jenny nodded. "You and your mother will know best how to tell them your news." After a brief pause, Jenny said, "Now I want to ask you several questions on some topics you are probably already thinking about. You don't have to make these decisions today. But it's important that you have an idea of what you're going to do before we talk to your mother."

"All right."

Jenny's tone was serious. "First, are you in any way considering an abortion?"

The question did not take Stephanie by surprise. "If you had asked me that question six months ago, I would have said, 'No way, never in a million years.' Even before I became

a Christian, I was dead set against abortion. But I wasn't pregnant then. Now I realize why so many girls get abortions. On the surface it seems like the easy answer to all my problems. It's scary how attractive abortion has appeared to me, especially in the last month."

Kate sounded alarmed. "Stephanie, you're not really thinking—"

"No, not at all," Stephanie cut in firmly. "I know abortion is wrong. I'm not going to make my mistake worse by disobeying God again. Besides, there is a living person inside me, and I am committed to loving both God and people. Abortion would not be the loving way to treat this person."

"I admire your commitment to love and obey God, Stephanie," Jenny said, "even though it's not the easy way out."

"Me too," Kate chimed in.

"But I would like you to make me a promise, Stephanie," Jenny added. "You may be pressured by Brent or his family or some of your relatives and friends to get an abortion. If you are ever tempted to take the easy way out, I want you to call me—anytime, night or day. Will you promise to do that?"

"Yes, I will," Stephanie answered with conviction. "Thanks for being willing to hold me accountable."

Jenny moved on to her next question. "Do you love Brent? Do you want to marry him?"

Stephanie frowned. "I don't think I love Brent at all. I hardly know him. Our relationship was childish and selfish, I suppose—

nothing to build a marriage on. Besides, he lives out west, and I live here. We don't have anything in common . . . except this." She touched her abdomen, which was beginning to make room for the fetus within.

"Would you consider raising the child yourself as a single parent?" Jenny said.

"I don't know," Stephanie said, searching the ceiling in thought. "I've always wanted to be a mother, and there are many things about having a child that appeal to me. But I haven't even finished high school yet. I don't have a job, and it's not fair to ask Mom to support us both. I also wonder if being raised by a working mom is really best for my child. I need to think about this more."

Jenny continued, "How would you feel about Brent or his parents raising your child, if they wanted to do so?"

Stephanie frowned again. "I don't even know his parents. If I gave the child up, I would want to make sure it would go to an excellent home."

"So you have already thought about adoption?" Kate interjected.

After a sigh, Stephanie said, "I know it's an option, but I need to learn more about it. And whatever I decide, I think Brent should have a vote."

"Then you're sure Brent is the father?" Jenny said.

Stephanie forced a humorless laugh. "The only time in my life I have sex, and I get pregnant. Yes, Brent is definitely the father."

Your 911 Response

Stephanie has some tough decisions to make, none of them easy. But she has two friends who have come alongside to help her carry the heavy load. We have discussed what it means to *be* a supportive friend. But what does *doing* support look like in your relationships with your friends?

Support in Action

There are a lot of ways that you can live out your support of your friends. One of the best ways to understand how to demonstrate support to others is to understand what support means to you.

Take a moment to think about the most stressful experience in your life during the last six months, a time when you really needed others to help you carry a heavy load of some kind.

Describe that experience. _____

_____

_____

_____

_____

Did someone come alongside you and provide needed support? ☐ **Yes** ☐ **No**

If yes, explain how this person(s) supported you. How did you feel when that person provided

needed support? _____

_____

_____

_____

If no, explain how you felt about carrying your burden alone. How would you have felt if some-

one had provided the support you needed? _____

_____

_____

_____

When you need support, how will a friend notice? In other words, what signals do you want your friend to pick up on which indicate that you would appreciate his or her support? For example, you might say, "When I am frustrated about something, I would like my friend to notice and ask how he or she could help me." Describe other ways you signal your need for support and how you would like your friend to respond.

_____

_____

_____

_____

Go and Do Likewise

Jesus said, "Do for others what you would like them to do for you" (Matt. 7:12). Applying this principle to support, Jesus is saying that you need to support others in the same way you

would like them to support you. That is a good guide for knowing what support should look like—it should look like what you want it to look like for you.

Prayer

Close by asking God to help you be a supportive friend to _____ (name of your friend) this week in the same way you desire others to support you.

_____

_____

_____

_____

_____

_____

_____

_____

_____

_____

A *911* Friend
Is Supportive

STEPHANIE'S STORY CONTINUES

Stephanie, Jenny, and Kate spent another hour talking through the many choices Stephanie would have to make regarding her baby's future. Kate and Jenny promised to be available to help her in any way they could: taking her to medical appointments, making arrangements for finishing school after the baby comes, and talking to adoption agencies if she chose to relinquish the baby.

Then Jenny helped Stephanie think through what she would say when they sat down with her mother later in the day to break the news. Finally, they joined hands in prayer again. Kate and Jenny asked God to fill Stephanie with His wisdom and perseverance through the months ahead and to help her with the immediate tasks of talking to her mother, father, brother, and Brent and his family.

Stephanie wished she could stay in the warm, supportive environment she had found at Jenny's house. But she knew what she had to do next. Kate had to go home and get ready for her Saturday afternoon job of cleaning offices with her brother. She promised to be praying for Stephanie. As she drove away, Stephanie got into Jenny's car, and they headed for the meeting with Stephanie's mother.

Stephanie felt terrible about the news she was bringing to her mother. Jenny had said that her parents would probably experience many of the same emotions she was struggling through: confusion, fear, guilt, and shame. They may even feel a sense of betrayal and anger over Stephanie's pregnancy. "Just like

you," Jenny had said as she drove Stephanie home, "your parents need time to adjust to the news of your pregnancy and its implications on their lives." Still, Stephanie wished she did not have to burden her mother with the news.

When the two of them arrived, Stephanie's mother, Claire, was getting ready to leave for a few errands. "Jenny and I need to talk to you about something, Mom," Stephanie said. "Can we sit down for a few minutes?" Appearing suspicious at her daughter's serious mood and Jenny's presence, Claire agreed. They sat around a small table in the breakfast nook.

After drawing a deep breath and releasing it slowly, Stephanie said, "I found out yesterday . . . that I'm . . . pregnant."

Claire's face clouded with disbelief. "You . . . you are pregnant? Stephanie, why. . . how . . . ?"

Stephanie summarized her encounter with Brent in June and the results of the pregnancy test yesterday afternoon. Her mother listened in stunned silence.

"Mom, I'm so sorry," she continued as warm tears trickled down her cheeks. "I never wanted this to happen. I made a terrible mistake. With Jenny's help, I have confessed my sin to God and asked for His forgiveness. But I know what I have done will be an embarrassment and an extra burden to you. Please forgive me."

Claire began to weep. "Of course I forgive you, Stephanie," she said. "I am shocked and disappointed and hurt, but I forgive you." Mother and daughter embraced, held each other, and cried together.

As Stephanie and her mother dabbed their eyes with tissues, Jenny said, "Claire,

Discovery Day

4

Stephanie and I have spent some time talking about the many implications of her pregnancy on her life and yours. She will need some time and your support to make all the decisions needed. But we thought it would be good for her to share with you what she is thinking so far." Then she nodded to Stephanie.

"First, I want you to know that I will not have an abortion," she stated firmly. "It's wrong, and I won't do it."

"I'm relieved to hear you say that, honey," Claire said. "And I know God is pleased with your decision, even though it leaves you with greater responsibility for dealing with the child."

Stephanie went on. "And I'm not planning to marry Brent, at least not now. We're not in love, and we're not mature enough for marriage. I think Brent will agree. I hope you will help me talk to Brent and his family when the time comes."

"Of course I will," Claire assured. "But what are your plans for the baby?"

Stephanie knew her answer to that question would deeply affect her mom, dad, and other family members. The baby would not only be her child, it would also be the first grandchild in the family. "I don't know yet," she answered. "I hope you will talk with me and pray with me about whether I should keep the baby or consider adoption. I know it will be the most difficult decision of my life so far. I want to take my time and be sure."

Claire nodded her agreement. "Thank you for including me. That means a lot to me."

The three of them continued to talk for almost an hour about many of the implications of Stephanie's pregnancy. She expressed her desire to continue classes at least for the fall term. Jenny suggested that Claire and Stephanie discuss the issue with school officials on Monday. They debated how best for Stephanie to tell her father and brother about the pregnancy, agreeing that a phone call later in the day would be sufficient. Stephanie said she would also call Brent this evening,

asking her mother to be with her when she did.

They spent a little time comparing the advantages and disadvantages of single parenthood and adoption. The discussion turned to Stephanie's goals for education and career and how these goals would be impacted by each option. Just before leaving, Jenny led in prayer for God's wisdom and guidance as Stephanie and Claire continued to sort through the options and implications of the pregnancy.

Stephanie was still awake at midnight, lying in her dark room, replaying the events of the day. There had been more tears when she talked to her father and then her brother Joe by telephone. Dad was disgusted and angry at the news, and Joe's "holier-than-thou" response made her feel like a tramp. Stephanie prayed that God would help her mend those relationships, which were very important to her.

Brent didn't believe the news until Stephanie gave him the phone number at the clinic, saying he could call Monday and talk to the doctor himself. Then he seemed so rattled that he didn't know what to say. Stephanie encouraged him to talk to his parents and call her in a few days.

For the last several minutes before falling asleep, Stephanie placed her hands on her tummy. She imagined what her baby looked like now and what it would look like at birth. Was it a boy or a girl? Would it look more like her or like Brent? Would this baby have a better opportunity for a happy, fulfilling life in the home of adoptive parents, or should she take responsibility for it no matter what the cost to her? Question after question appeared, but there were no answers.

Stephanie's last thought of the day was a peaceful one. She was not alone in her difficult and painful circumstance. Thanks to Jenny Shaw, Kate, and her understanding mother, she knew she would have all the support she needed to get through the next seven months and beyond.

Your 911 Response

A girl struggling through an unplanned pregnancy needs a lot of support. She has many tough decisions to make. Most of your friends do not have problems and decisions this serious. But they *do* have problems and decisions, and they need your support. Being a supportive 911 friend can get rather time consuming. How much of your limited time should you invest in supporting your friends? Are you responsible to help everyone who needs support? Should you help only a select few and no more?

How a 911 Friend Should Feel Toward Others

One day an expert in religious law asked Jesus what he must do to receive eternal life. Jesus asked him what the law of Moses said, and the man answered:

> "You must love the Lord your God with all your heart, all your soul, all your strength, and all your mind. And, 'Love your neighbor as yourself'" (Luke 10:27).

When Jesus told him he had answered correctly, the man asked him, "Who is my neighbor?" Open your Bible and read Jesus' answer in Luke 10:30–37.

A Jewish man was attacked by bandits, stripped of his clothes and money, and left beaten and half-dead beside the road.

Who were the first two people to come by, and what did they do?

_____

_____

_____

_____

A Samaritan man came by to help. But Samaritans were despised by most of the Jews. Write below the one verse that describes what the Samaritan man did for the beaten Jewish traveler.

_____

_____

_____

_____

When Jesus asked the religious law expert which of the three men was a neighbor to the beaten man. "The man replied, 'The one who showed him mercy.' Then Jesus said, 'Yes, now go and do the same'" (Luke 10:37).

The Samaritan showed mercy. He certainly came alongside and helped the man in need. But why? What caused the Samaritan to do what he did? Write down Luke 10:33.

_____

When the Samaritan saw his neighbor in need, he felt compassion and deep pity. That's what a 911 friend feels for those in need: compassion and a deep longing to help. A compassionate friend does not keep count of to whom or how often he or she supplies needed support. A compassionate heart simply wants to help those in need. Do you have a compassionate heart that moves you to help others?

The Motivation to Help Others

Do you jump out of bed every morning excitedly asking yourself, *Who needs my help and support today?* Probably not. We all tend to need more motivation and compassion for the ministry of sharing support with others. The apostle James must have run into some people who were lacking in the compassion department, because he wrote:

> "Suppose you see a brother or sister who needs food or clothing, and you say, 'Well, good-bye and God bless you, stay warm and eat well'—but then you don't give that person any food or clothing. What good does that do?" (James 2:15–16).

Where do we get the motivation we need to provide support? How would you feel if the friend who needed your support was Jesus Christ Himself? Would that spark your motivation and compassion? Imagine leaving the home of a friend you have just helped in some way, and someone taps you on the shoulder. You turn around to find Jesus standing there. He says, "Thank you very much for taking the time to help Me. Your compassion and support mean so much to Me." Would that blow you away? If you knew you would get that same response from Christ every time, would you be more highly motivated to share support with your friends?

Read the following verses from Matthew 25 carefully. Jesus is explaining how He will welcome believers into His kingdom. And then He says this:

> "'For I was hungry, and you fed me. I was thirsty, and you gave me a drink. I was a stranger, and you invited me into your home. I was naked, and you gave me clothing. I was sick, and you cared for me. I was in prison, and you visited me.'

> "Then these righteous ones will reply, 'Lord, when did we ever see you hungry and feed you? Or thirsty and give you something to drink? Or a stranger and show you hospitality? Or naked and give you clothing? When did we ever see you sick or in prison, and visit you?' And the King will tell them, 'I assure you, when you did it to one of the least of these my brothers and sisters, you were doing it to me!'" (Matt. 25:35–40).

Did you know that when you provide helpful support to others, you are doing it to Jesus?

 ❏ **Yes** ❏ **No**

How do you respond to this truth?

_____

_____

_____

_____

Jesus goes on to say to nonbelievers:

"For I was hungry, and you didn't feed me. I was thirsty, and you didn't give me anything to drink. I was a stranger, and you didn't invite me into your home. I was naked, and you gave me no clothing. I was sick and in prison, and you didn't visit me.'

"Then they will reply, 'Lord when did we ever see you hungry or thirsty or a stranger or naked or sick or in prison, and not help you?' And he will answer, 'I assure you, when you refused to help the least of these my brothers and sisters, you were refusing to help me.'" (Matt. 25:42–45).

Did you know that when you fail to provide helpful support to others that you are failing to support Jesus?   ❑ **Yes**   ❑ **No**

How do you respond to this truth?

_____

_____

_____

Does it increase your desire to help others when you realize that your actions will directly affect Jesus?

Prayer

Ask God to give you a greater heart of compassion.

_____

_____

_____

_____

_____

_____

A *911* Friend
Is Available
STEPHANIE'S STORY CONTINUES

Stephanie waited until she and Jenny were in the car to tell the latest news. Claire had to work at the market today, so Jenny had volunteered to drive Stephanie to her scheduled sixth-month prenatal examination.

Placing a hand on her ballooning tummy, Stephanie announced, "It's a girl. The images were clear this month, they said. Everything looks good. The baby is healthy and growing."

"A girl! That's wonderful," Jenny said with guarded enthusiasm. "Are you doing OK?"

"Me? Yes, I'm doing well. The doctor says I'm a couple of pounds overweight, but she wasn't worried about it."

"I mean are you OK emotionally, knowing that the baby is a girl?" Jenny pressed. "Does it make you want to change your mind?"

Stephanie thought about it for a moment. "I had a hunch that it was a girl, so I'm pleased about that. There is still a part of me that would love to take care of my little girl. But Mom and I prayed about this a lot, talked a lot, and cried a lot. I'm convinced that the best thing for the baby is to grow up with a mother and father who love her and can take care of her. We are going ahead with our plans to share her with a loving family."

"And Brent and his parents feel OK about that?" Jenny said.

"Yes. It might be different if the father was someone I was already planning to marry. But Brent and I are not going to be together; we both know that. And it might be different if I was mature enough to raise the child by myself, but I'm not. His family and mine agree that the baby deserves a better home than either Brent or I can provide."

Jenny drove in silence for a minute. "I really admire you, Stephanie, for putting the baby's welfare above your own desires."

The affirmation warmed Stephanie. "Thanks, but I couldn't have done it without people like you and Mom and Kate. Your support has made our decision easier."

Jenny nodded her appreciation for the comment. Then she said, "How is school going?"

"Very well. I plan to stay in class almost until my due date. Then I'll home-school until the baby comes. I should be back in school in a couple of weeks so I can graduate with my class."

"I'm really happy for you, Stephanie," Jenny said. "Everything seems to be working out."

Stephanie hummed her agreement. "Romans 8:28 has been very special to me in the last few months. God is bringing good out of my not-so-good situation and the consequences I am facing."

Jenny smiled. "That's the best news of all, Stephanie."

Your 911 Response

According to Matthew 25:35–40, Kate and Jenny were loving and supporting Christ as they shared their love and support with their friend Stephanie. When you compassionately support your friend, you are doing it to Christ.

Walk through Discovery Day Five with your friendship partner by following the directions below.

Being Support to Each Other

Matthew 25:35-40 indicates that as you express your availability, acceptance, comfort, and support to your friend, you also do so to Christ. Take a few moments and tell each other how this makes you feel and how it motivates you to be a better friend. Write down what you share.

_____

_____

_____

_____

We all need support at various times. Ask your friend how you can be a better supportive friend to him or her in the future. Write down your friend's response here. Then answer the same question as your friend writes your response in his or her workbook.

_____

_____

_____

_____

Take turns answering these questions to each other:

Is it sometimes difficult for you to ask for my help when you need it? Is it difficult for you to accept my help when I offer it? Do you have these difficulties with other friends? If so, why do you think you respond that way?

_____

_____

_____

_____

Sometimes people feel they shouldn't need others to help them. Do you tend to feel this way? If so, take turns discussing how you can help each other overcome the resistance to accept support and help from others.

_____

_____

Together, identify other friends in your youth group or elsewhere that you both sense could use your support this week. List their names here and describe the kind of support they need and why.

_____

_____

_____

_____

Detail specific ways each of you plans to show support to the friends you listed above.

_____

_____

_____

_____

Prayer

Close in prayer, asking God to empower you to minister support to others this week. Tell Jesus how you are honored to minister to Him as you minister to those around you.

_____

_____

_____

_____

_____

_____

_____

The PROJECT 911 Collection

The story of Stephanie in this week's workbook is adapted from the small book entitled *My Friend Is Struggling with an Unplanned Pregnancy*. The book is designed as a giveaway book you can read and then give to a friend who is going through that situation. Beyond the fictional story, this book provides guidance for the many decisions that need to be made, none of which is easy.

If you want one or more of these books for a friend, contact your youth leader. He or she may have a number of copies on hand. If not, this and other books in this collection can be ordered in bulk by calling 1-800-933-9673 ext. 9-2039. Or you can purchase copies of this book at your local Christian bookstore.

WEEK FIVE

A *911* Friend Is Encouraging

JESSICA'S STORY

ifteen-year-old Jessica Ingram knew what this evening's "family meeting" was about, even though Mom would not tell her anything specific. Jessica's sister, Karen, and brother, Mark, knew too. You would have to be blind, deaf, and brainless not to understand what was going on. Dad and Mom would announce to their three children tonight that their "trial separation" had not worked and that they were getting a divorce.

The "divorce meeting" tonight would be as horrible as the "separation meeting" had been three months ago, Jessica knew. She would rather dive into a vat of acid and disappear forever than be here tonight. Not literally, of course. She had not even had thoughts of suicide. But what was the point of an Ingram family meeting when everyone would go away feeling even worse than they felt now? Why glorify a divorce by sitting down at the dinner table to announce it?

Flopped across her bed, Jessica turned up the volume on her CD headphones so she could not hear the silence in the house. Her eighteen-year-old sister, Karen, would be home from work in a half-hour, just before the dreaded dinner meeting. If she were home now, Karen would be storming around the house slamming doors and cupboards and biting everybody's heads off. Venting, she called it. Karen was always very up-front with her anger about Mom and Dad's breakup, beginning in the middle of the separation meeting back in April. At least when Karen was venting, Jessica felt a little better. The silence was awful.

Their twelve-year-old brother, Mark, was at home, but he was the exact opposite of Karen. After the separation meeting, Mom asked Mark how he was doing. He just shrugged and went back to his computer games, acting as if nothing had happened. He was probably in his room right now with his own headphones on, systematically annihilating the evil warriors of the Planet Zarg on his computer. Jessica knew the family crisis was affecting him, but the kid was just blocking out his feelings or something. She was afraid of what might happen when it all caught up with him.

Mom was home too, Jessica knew, but she was buried in a corner of the house with one of her romance novels. Jessica thought she would feel better if her mother were in here ragging on her to clean up her room or do her chores. But Mom was apparently in retreat mode like she and Mark.

Dad was *not* home, of course. After the separation meeting, he had moved into an apartment four miles away. Dad was bringing a couple of pizzas for dinner tonight, Mom had said. Jessica wrinkled her nose at the thought. What a cruel joke to sit down and casually eat pizza while dismantling the family. Jessica wasn't hungry. She hadn't been hungry for three months. She hadn't slept well either, bothered by an itchy skin rash and horrible nightmares. It all started in April. If this is how she felt after the separation, how much worse would it be when Mom and Dad were finally divorced? She didn't want to know.

As the music pounded in her ears, Jessica tried to pray. She had been a Christian almost a year now, having trusted Christ last summer at church youth camp. She had noticed a positive

Discovery Day

1

difference in her life since meeting Jesus. Prayer, Bible study, and worship were now significant parts of her life. But so far that difference had not extended to her family—particularly her parents. They only attended church about once every two months, when the youth music team, with Jessica singing, was on the program. And her parents had drifted further apart in the past year, even though Jessica prayed for them regularly.

Praying for her parents' reconciliation now seemed almost hopeless. For one thing, Jessica assumed that the breakup was partly her fault. She could have been more obedient, compliant, and helpful, especially before becoming a Christian. Her stubborn behavior at times had made her parents' lives more difficult, she knew. Jessica had asked God many times to forgive her for not being a better kid. With Dad's arrival less than an hour away, Jessica mainly prayed for Mark and Karen—and herself.

The divorce meeting was a sham of family life. Dad and Mark shoveled down pizza and talked about baseball like it was a party. Jessica, Karen, and Mom took courtesy bites then pushed their plates away and sat in silence. Mom seemed on the verge of tears. Karen had fire in her eyes and looked like a ticking time bomb ready to explode. Jessica just wanted it to be over so she could go back to her room.

"Your mother and I have something to tell you," Dad announced finally. "Our problems have gotten worse instead of better since I moved out. The separation and counseling haven't helped. So we have decided to get a divorce. We want you kids to know that this is not about you; it's about Mom and me. We both love all three of you, and we will—"

Karen jumped to her feet so quickly that her chair toppled backward and hit the hardwood floor with a crash. "This is so sick!" she screamed at both parents. "If you really loved us, you wouldn't do this to us. Why can't you work things out? I don't think you're really trying. I don't think you *want* to try." Spiced with

some strong words Jessica had never heard her sister use before, Karen vented big-time. Dad tried to interrupt a couple of times, but it was like spitting into the wind. So he just sat there and took it. Jessica knew Karen's outburst wouldn't change his mind. Mom squeezed her eyes closed and cried silently. Mark occupied himself by nibbling on pizza crust.

The more Karen blazed, the more Jessica could feel her own anger and hurt. Karen said things she wished she could say. It was like her older sister was venting for both of them. And when Karen started crying, Jessica felt a lump in her throat and a warm tear on her cheek. Even though she could not agree with everything Karen said or how she said it, Jessica envied her sister's ability to blow off steam.

In less than two minutes—which seemed like two hours to Jessica—it was all over. Dad said his piece, and Karen exploded. Then Dad explained that he and Mom were still discussing living arrangements—who would live with whom and for how long. This was a new problem for Jessica. Dad had moved out and left the kids with Mom. Karen had told Jessica that she was pretty sure Dad was already dating, and that he probably wouldn't want the girls or Mark living with him, for obvious reasons. Now Dad was talking about splitting up the Ingram family even more. And he was looking at Jessica when he said, "Maybe when school starts in September, someone would like to come live with me."

Jessica wasn't about to choose between her parents, but neither was she ready to become a Ping-Pong ball bouncing between them. Her room and her stuff were here. Jessica felt her place was with her mother, Karen, and Mark. She didn't know how she would tell her dad that she wanted to stay with Mom.

Jessica's father had a business appointment at 7:30, so he left a few minutes after 7:00. Jessica loved her dad, but she was glad to see him go. She had had enough of "family unity" for one night.

Your 911 Response

You may know someone like Jessica whose parents are splitting up or who have already gotten a divorce. You may have even gone through a similar ordeal yourself. Others you know in this situation really need a 911 friend. They can use someone who will care, be interested, listen, and be a safe zone. They can also benefit from your acceptance, affirmation, and support. Another thing they can use is some encouragement. This not only applies to problems at home. At sometime or another, everyone needs to be encouraged.

What Is Encouragement?

Circle any words or phrases below that relate to being encouraged.

* A splitting headache
* Angry
* Looking on the bright side

* Spirits lifted
* Moody
* Cheered up

* Feeling more positive
* Confused all the time

"So encourage each other and build each other up, just as you are already doing" (1 Thess. 5:11).

"Think of ways to encourage one another to outbursts of love and good deeds" (Heb. 10:24).

How would you define *encouragement* in your own words?

Encouragement is . . . _____

_____

_____

Encouragement means lifting people's spirits and cheering them up by helping them focus on the positive and good things in life.

Imagine that your day goes like this:

7:45 A.M.:   You miss your ride to school, so your mother has to take you. All the way to school she lectures you about punctuality.

8:12 A.M.:   You confess to your first-period teacher that you left your assignment at home, so she writes your name on the chalkboard under the heading "No Clue."

11:47 A.M.:   You carry your lunch to the table where your friends are sitting, but there isn't a chair for you—and nobody moves to let you in.

2:06 P.M.:   Someone slips you a note from your boyfriend or girlfriend that says, "I never want to see you again." The note is taped to a small bottle of mouthwash.

4:33 P.M.:   Your dad forgets to come to your game—again. But it doesn't really matter because the coach won't let you play anyway—again.

After your lousy day, what would encourage you? Check (✔) any experiences below that would lift your spirits and help you see the bright side of life.

❑ A friend says, "You think *you* have problems. Let me tell you about mine" (blah, blah, blah).

❑ A friend explains, "Here's why that happened, Dummy, and here's what you need to do so it doesn't happen again" (blah, blah, blah).

❑ You receive e-mail from a friend that says, "Sorry to hear about your discouraging day. I'm praying for you."

❑ A friend phones you to say, "What's your problem? You know this wouldn't have happened to you unless God was punishing you for something. So what have you done wrong?"

❑ A friend shows up with a hot new Christian music CD. "I heard you had a tough day. I thought we could listen to this together."

Prayer

Thank God for the friends who are sources of encouragement to you. Ask Him to help you be an encouragement to someone this week.

_____

_____

_____

_____

_____

_____

_____

_____

A **911** Friend Is Encouraging

JESSICA'S STORY CONTINUES

**K**aren helped Mom clean up after dinner, Mark beamed back to Planet Zarg on his computer, and Jessica slipped away to her room and headphones. She knew Mom and Karen would rehash all the gory details of the evening. It was the last thing Jessica wanted to do. A divorce was something that should be decided in private and then buried there, she decided. It's not something you chat about, like how you liked a movie. And it's not something you talk about with friends, like, "I just got a new pair of Nikes on sale, and my parents are getting a divorce."

Jessica was suddenly aware of one benefit of being a Christian she had not previously realized. Her best friends were church friends, including the adult leaders, Doug and Jenny Shaw. And since none of her friends knew her family, they would not hear about the divorce unless she told them—which she would not. Even her best friend, Natalie Simmons, who had invited her to church camp a year ago and prayed with Jessica when she trusted Christ, knew only that her parents were separated. It would be important that Natalie help her keep the divorce a secret. But, of course, Natalie had to know about the divorce if she was going to help keep it a secret. So Jessica decided to tell her—and only her.

"Going to Natalie's, back by ten," Jessica called out to her mother on the way out the door. She was on her bike and headed down the driveway before her mother could respond. It felt good to be outside on a warm summer evening. It felt even better to be away from the house where the aroma of pizza kept reminding her of Dad's announcement. She wondered if she would ever be able to eat pizza again.

"Your parents are getting divorced? Oh, Jessie, I'm so sorry." Natalie's words took Jessica by surprise. There was so much feeling in them, so much love, and not an ounce of blame. The two girls had biked over to the city park and were sitting in adjoining swings when Jessica told Natalie about the dinner meeting at her house.

"Thanks, but it's a secret, all right?" Jessica responded.

"A secret? What do you mean?"

"I mean I don't want anybody at church to know," Jessica said insistently. "And now that you know, I don't even want to talk about it anymore."

"But why, Jessie?" Natalie probed.

Jessica hesitated, wavering on how honest she should be. Having told Natalie everything so far, she decided to be up-front with her, even though it was difficult. "Because . . . because . . . the Ingram family isn't normal, all right? My parents are not Christians, and I'm not proud of the fact that they are doing this. I'd rather people didn't know." Then Jessica pushed herself back and lifted her feet to swing. Natalie did the same, and the two girls glided silently side by side for several minutes.

When the swings were almost still again, Natalie said, "What about Jenny Shaw?" Jenny was also present when Jessica trusted Christ last summer. Jenny had discipled Jessica one-on-one for several weeks after camp.

Discovery Day

"What *about* Jenny?" Jessica asked.

"She's a spiritual big sister to you," Natalie returned. "You said so yourself. I think you should tell Jenny what's going on at home. She could probably help you deal with your parents' divorce."

"I *am* dealing with it, Natalie. I'm just dealing with it . . . well . . . more privately than other people do."

"A divorce is a very big thing to handle privately," Natalie said, sounding a little like a big sister herself.

"I told *you,* didn't I?"

"Yes, and I'm going to be praying for you," Natalie assured. "I'm your friend, and I'm here for you. But I think Jenny may be able to help you deal with your emotions better than I can."

"Emotions? I'm not the emotional one in the family. That happens to be my sister, Karen." Jessica didn't want to argue with Natalie. But she didn't like her friend telling her what she needed, even if she was right.

Natalie was silent for a minute, causing Jessica to wonder if she had given up. Then she said, "Remember when my older brother was killed two years ago?"

Jessica thought about it. "I barely knew you then. It was an accident at work, right?"

Natalie nodded. "Skip's death rocked the whole family pretty hard. I thought the best way to handle it was to get back to normal as soon as possible. So I told myself to get over it and get on with life. I didn't realize that there is a natural grieving process I had to go through. Jenny and Doug helped me get my feelings out so I could deal with them."

Jessica waited for the punch line, but Natalie said nothing more. She didn't have to. *A divorce is like a death,* Jessica thought. *You need to grieve it; you need to pour your feelings out to someone who can help you deal with them. Jenny is your spiritual big sister. You need to go see her.*

After a few more minutes of silent swinging, Jessica said, "I'd better get home. I'm worried about Mark. I need to spend some time with him."

Before getting on their bikes, Natalie gave Jessica a long hug. "I really hurt for you, Jessie. I'm so sorry you have to go through this."

Jessica returned the hug. "Thanks. Thanks for caring."

Jessica didn't take the most direct route home. She wanted to think a little more about whether or not she should tell Jenny Shaw about one of the saddest days in her life.

Your 911 Response

Jessica has a good friend in Natalie, someone she can talk to about her problems, someone who is there to care and listen, comfort, accept, support, and encourage her. Some of your friends may not be as open about their discouragement as Jessica is with Natalie. And some people are pretty good at covering up their struggles, so you can't always tell how they feel just by looking at them. You need to keep your eyes and ears open for the signs of discouragement, then allow God to involve you in being the encouragement your friend needs at the time.

As we have been discovering, there is a time and a place for every act or expression of 911 friendship. Lifting a friend's spirits with cheery thoughts and words may be helpful sometimes, but at other times your friend may need another expression of your care. The Bible tells us to use our words to build people up and be helpful to them "according to the need of the moment, that [you] may give grace to those who hear" (Eph. 4:29 NASB). It is important to know what your friend needs at the moment so you know how to be a friend to him or her.

What Is the Need of the Moment?

For each scenario below, check (✔) the response that you feel best meets your friend's "need of the moment." Then fill in the blank with the quality of friendship he or she needs at that moment: available, accepting, affirming, supportive, or encouraging. *NOTE: You will need to list one of these friendship qualities twice in this exercise.*

Your friend tells you with excitement that he or she just aced a final exam.

My friend needs: ❑ a tranquilizer   ❑ someone to be excited with him or her

❑ to get a grip on his   ❑ to put life into perspective
or her emotions

My friend needs me to be a/an _____ friend by identifying with his or her joy.

(a) available; (b) accepting; (c) affirming; (d) supportive; or (e) encouraging

Your friend seems discouraged about something, but hasn't said anything.

My friend needs: ❑ medication   ❑ to get over it

❑ someone to care enough   ❑ to know that no one likes a loser
to listen and be a safe zone

My friend needs me to be a/an _____ friend who will be there to care, listen, and be a safe zone.

(a) available; (b) accepting; (c) affirming; (d) supportive; or (e) encouraging

Your friend feels rejected by others on the team because his or her mistake cost them a game.

My friend needs: ❑ to practice harder   ❑ to be valued for who he or she is,
regardless of performance

❑ to tell his or her team   ❑ to never play sports again
members to change
their attitudes

My friend needs me to be a/an _____ friend who loves people for who they are, not for how they perform.

(a) available; (b) accepting; (c) affirming; (d) supportive; or (e) encouraging

Your friend has just suffered a serious loss and is really hurting.

My friend needs: ❑ someone to hurt with him   ❑ to stuff the hurt and get on with life
or her

❑ to take pain medication   ❑ to hide somewhere and hurt alone

My friend needs me to be a/an _____ friend who will identify with the hurt to provide comfort.

(a) available; (b) accepting; (c) affirming; (d) supportive; or (e) encouraging

My friend is struggling in a class and needs to study hard for a big exam.

My friend needs: ❑ to get smarter   ❑ to learn how to cheat without
                                                       getting caught

                  ❑ someone to help him or   ❑ to sign up for easier classes
                     her study for the exam

My friend needs me to be a/an _____ friend to come alongside and help him
or her carry this burden.

   (a) available; (b) accepting; (c) affirming; (d) supportive; or (e) encouraging

My friend is feeling a little down because he or she can't be with a boyfriend/girlfriend this
weekend.

My friend needs: ❑ to break up with the   ❑ to spend time this weekend
                     boyfriend/girlfriend   cleaning his or her room

                  ❑ someone to cheer him   ❑ to be left alone to deal with
                     or her up   his or her sadness

My friend needs me to be a/an _____ friend to cheer him or her up to lift his
or her spirits.

   (a) available; (b) accepting; (c) affirming; (d) supportive; or (e) encouraging

Did you select each of the following correct answers in exercises 1 through 6 above?

1. an **affirming** friend	❑ **Yes**	❑ **No**
2. an **available** friend	❑ **Yes**	❑ **No**
3. an **accepting** friend	❑ **Yes**	❑ **No**
4. an **affirming** friend	❑ **Yes**	❑ **No**
5. a **supportive** friend	❑ **Yes**	❑ **No**
6. an **encouraging** friend	❑ **Yes**	❑ **No**

As you are better able to detect your friend's needs at the moment, you are better able to be
the 911 friend he or she needs.

Prayer

Praise God today that He is your best friend, always available, affirming, accepting, supportive, and encouraging to you.

   "Why am I discouraged? Why so sad? I will put my hope in God! I will praise him again—
   my Savior and my God" (Ps. 42:11).

_____

_____

_____

_____

_____

A 911 Friend Is Encouraging

JESSICA'S STORY CONTINUES

It took most of Friday morning for Jessica to work up the courage to call Jenny Shaw. She felt stupid about her hesitation, because Jenny had been nothing but a kind, supportive, and encouraging friend ever since they met at camp last summer. Still, Jessica felt a little embarrassed to tell Jenny about her parents' divorce. But Natalie had encouraged her to do so, and she trusted her friend's judgment.

When she finally dialed Jenny's number—and fought off the urge to hang up before she answered—Jessica knew she had done the right thing. Without telling Jenny anything specific, Jessica asked if they could meet together soon to "talk about something kind of important." Jenny said she could get away from the quick-print store tomorrow afternoon. It was supposed to be sunny and in the low 90s, so Jenny suggested they put on their swimsuits and lay out by the river. Jessica agreed, and Jenny promised to pick her up a little after 1:00.

The next afternoon, Jessica waited to tell her story until they had spread a blanket on the grassy riverside knoll and slathered each other with lotion. Sitting on the blanket to soak in the sun, they were close enough to the river to see the children playing at the water's edge but far enough away from people to talk freely without being overheard.

Jessica didn't know how to start, so she just blurted out, "My parents are getting a divorce."

Jenny reacted in near shock. "Oh, Jessie, no," she said with a pained expression, placing a comforting hand on Jessica's arm. "I hadn't heard. I didn't know."

"Nobody knew, except Natalie," Jessica explained. "I didn't want anybody to know. Natalie said I should talk to you."

"I'm so sorry, Jessie. This has to be very difficult for you."

Jessica could hear the comfort in Jenny's voice and feel the concern coming through her touch. She was already glad she had decided to share her news with Jenny. "It's been really . . . different . . . around our house," she admitted.

"Oh, Jessica, I really hurt for you," Jenny said. She seemed on the verge of tears, which brought a lump to Jessica's throat. "If you want to tell me about it, I'm here to listen."

Jessica didn't realize how ready she was to tell someone about her parents' conflict, separation, and impending divorce. For the next twenty minutes, she poured out the story. There had been no screaming or fighting, she explained. The breakup may have been easier to accept if there had been. Her mom and dad had just silently drifted apart. They seemed to live in two separate worlds, even when they were home together. Dad had his demanding business schedule, golf, and service club activities. Mom lived in a fantasy world of romance novels, home-and-garden magazines, soap operas, and syrupy TV dramas. Mr. and Mrs. Ingram had so little in common, Jessica figured, that they would be happier living apart.

She held it together emotionally until she started talking about the living arrangements for the fall. "I think Dad wants either me or Karen to live with him," she said, starting to cry, "but I don't want our family split up even more. I love Dad, but I belong with Mom and Karen and Mark. I don't know what to do. I don't want this to happen."

Discovery Day

3

Jessica didn't want to cry in public, even though there wasn't anyone near enough to pay attention. She tried to get a grip on her emotions. But when she felt Jenny's arm around her and saw the tears in her eyes, she couldn't hold back. "It's OK, Jessie. Go ahead and cry," Jenny said. "I know it hurts a lot. I'm so sorry. I'm here. Let it all out." With Jenny's encouragement, Jessica sobbed for a full minute. It was the first time she had cried about her parents' breakup.

Wiping her eyes with a beach towel, Jessica began to feel some of the fire she had seen in Karen. The burst of tears had seemingly unlocked the gates to her emotions. "Why did Dad and Mom have to do this to us?" she demanded angrily. "It's not right, it's not fair, especially to Mark." The thought of her brother suffering in silence brought another brief surge of tears.

Jenny just held her and spoke reassuringly. "It hurts me that you have to go through this, Jessie, because I really care for you. But we can get through it together. I'm going to be here for you." Then she prayed the sweetest prayer that made Jessica feel that Jenny really was her older sister.

In a few minutes they were dabbing their eyes, blowing their noses, and even joking a little about how they must look to anyone glancing their way. Then Jenny said, "Would it be OK if we meet again—maybe a few times—to talk about how to process your feelings about the divorce and get through the grief?"

"You mean, meet for breakfast and Bible study like we did last year after I trusted Christ?"

"Sure, if you're willing."

Jessica exulted inside. The time she had spent with Jenny after camp greatly helped her solidify her commitment to follow Christ and start on a path of spiritual growth. "Yes, I'd like that a lot," she said. Jessica and Jenny decided to meet the next two Saturday mornings for breakfast, with an option to add other Saturdays if needed. Then, leaving their towels on the blanket, they hurried down the knoll to cool off in the river.

Your 911 Response

You know what it's like to be discouraged, and your friends do too. Like Jessica, everyone has experienced painful experiences in life and has needed comfort, affirmation, acceptance, support, and encouragement.

In this Discovery Day and the two that follow, we will pull together everything we have discovered about being a 911 friend. Remember: Knowing what it means to be a true friend just in our heads is not enough; you need to experience true friendship so your relationships with others will deepen. So check out your progress by walking through the five qualities of friendship we have covered so far.

Experiencing Availability in Friendship

Being an **available** friend to others means that you express interest in them, carefully listen to them, and become a confidential safe zone for them.

Briefly describe how you were an available friend to someone recently (perhaps your friendship partner).

_____

_____

_____

_____

What was the reward or benefit of this experience? How did that experience help your friend?

_____

_____

_____

_____

Briefly describe how someone (perhaps your friendship partner) was an available friend to you recently and how that helped you.

_____

_____

_____

_____

Experiencing Acceptance in Friendship

Being an **accepting** friend means considering others worthy for who they are, regardless of what they have, how they look, or what they do.

Briefly describe how you were an accepting friend to someone recently (perhaps to your friendship partner).

_____

_____

_____

_____

What was the reward or benefit of this experience? How did it help your friend?

_____

_____

_____

_____

Briefly describe how someone (perhaps your friendship partner) was an accepting friend to you recently and how that helped you.

_____

_____

_____

_____

Confirm the Meeting Time with Your Friendship Partner

Contact your Friendship Partner to confirm your meeting time to go over Discovery Day Five.

_____(date); _____(time);

_____(place).

Prayer

Take a moment to thank God for the deepened friendship you are experiencing with your friendship partner. Ask Christ to help you continue to apply His truth about friendship in your life. If you have been hindered in experiencing true friendship, ask God to help you overcome your hindrances.

_____

_____

_____

_____

_____

_____

_____

_____

A **911** Friend Is Encouraging

JESSICA'S STORY CONTINUES

or the first time since her parents' separation, Jessica did not feel alone in her pain and sadness. During the next week, she received encouraging phone calls and e-mail from Jenny. And Natalie called or dropped in occasionally just to say she was praying for her. It was difficult that first week, knowing that the divorce would soon be final. She also hurt for Karen and Mark who were struggling in their own ways. But Jessica seemed better able to cope, knowing that two very special people outside her family cared about her and were upholding her. And she hoped that the comfort and encouragement she had found in her mentor and friend would equip her to help her brother and sister.

As soon as they sat down at the pancake house for their first meeting, Jenny asked Jessica, "How did it go this week?"

Jessica shrugged. "All right, I guess. It's still hard to accept my parents getting a divorce. I'm glad you told me about the grieving process. I think I have been experiencing denial and a little depression this week."

"That's why I wanted us to get together a couple of times," Jenny said. "The best way to work through those experiences is to talk about them and focus on what is happening behind the feelings."

After they ordered breakfast, Jenny pulled a sheet of paper from her purse and passed it over to Jessica. "The other day I was thinking about how you might be feeling about the divorce," she began. "So I started writing down a number of different feelings that may apply. Are there any on this list you have experienced?"

Jessica read the first word aloud, "'Disbelief,'" and stopped. "I can sure identify with that one. I can't believe my parents are getting a divorce. I really don't *want* to believe it. One night last week I dreamed that Dad was back home again, and everything was all right between him and Mom. It was so real that I got up in the morning almost expecting to find Dad at the kitchen table drinking coffee and reading the paper. But, of course, he wasn't there."

"Disbelief is a form of denial," Jenny informed. "It's the brain's way of trying to maintain a level of stability in the face of great stress. Some people show their denial by refusing to talk about a problem or even to admit there is a problem. Some may admit there is a problem but deny that they are affected by it. Denial is a defense mechanism, but it usually isn't healthy. Eventually you must admit that the divorce is happening and that your life will be different because of it."

Jessica nodded slowly. "I understand. Living in a dream world isn't healthy, and it isn't right. You can't deal with a problem effectively if you deny that it exists."

"That's an important insight, Jessie," Jenny said.

"I'm afraid Mark has slipped into denial big-time," Jessica added. "He won't talk about Mom and Dad. Whenever I bring up the subject, he retreats to his video games."

"Maybe God will use you to help him," Jenny said. "I have been praying for Mark and Karen just as I have been praying for you."

Discovery Day

4

WEEK FIVE

Jenny kept reading the list aloud. "'Shame,' 'embarrassment,' 'anger,' 'false guilt'—hm, I guess I have been feeling a little guilty too."

"Tell me about it."

Jessica hesitated at the painful thought. The waitress arrived with glasses of juice, and Jessica was grateful for a few extra seconds to frame her answer. "I think Mom and Dad's problems are partly my fault. I haven't always been a model child at home. When I turned thirteen, I felt pretty independent. So one night I violated my curfew—on purpose—by about a half-hour. I got into a big argument with my parents about it when I got home. I remember Dad shouting, 'You make it very hard on your mother and me when you do things like this, Jessica. Marriage isn't easy, and your behavior doesn't make it any easier.' That's when I realized they weren't getting along very well and that I might be part of the problem."

"It saddens me to hear that you feel responsible for your parents' breakup," Jenny said compassionately, "and I can see how you might feel that way. But you are not to blame. You may not be a model child, but no child is. Parents have to deal with life's difficulties, including disagreements with their children. Your parents are responsible for their relationship."

"But Dad said—"

Jenny quickly interrupted. "Your dad may find it hard to accept full responsibility for his problems. A lot of people do. He probably didn't mean to hurt you by it, but pointing to your misbehavior allowed him to shift some of the blame away from himself."

Jessica pondered Jenny's words for a moment. "So it's not my fault after all?"

"No, the breakup is not your fault, and getting your parents back together is not your responsibility. They are adults. They are responsible for their relationship. All you can do is pray for them and love them."

Jessica sat back and released a long sigh. "That's kind of a relief."

"It should be," Jenny said. "You don't have to feel guilty anymore."

The waitress arrived with two orders of pancakes. As they ate, Jessica continued reading through Jenny's list and noted a few more feelings she had experienced. Jenny's insightful questions and comments helped her defuse some of the pain behind the feelings.

Jenny also asked how the rest of Jessica's life was going. Jessica sheepishly admitted that she felt so bummed out that she had ignored most of her chores around the house. She was hopelessly behind on the laundry and gardening, which were her responsibilities. Jenny surprised her by pulling out a cell phone and dialing Natalie right then. In less than two minutes, Jenny had arranged for Natalie to come over later in the day to help Jessica catch up on her chores.

After getting past a flash of embarrassment, Jessica sensed a wave of relief. Usually very good about keeping up with her work, she had been feeling too down to stay busy. Knowing that Natalie was coming to help her seemed to lift that weight off her shoulders.

The time flew by quickly, and Jenny had to leave for work. But they agreed to meet again next Saturday to continue their chat. Jessica left the pancake house that day grateful for Jenny's loving concern and practical help and very hopeful for the week ahead.

Your 911 Response

Jessica is blessed to have a couple of friends who are demonstrating their affirmation, support, and encouragement. These are expressions of true friendship. Let's continue to assess your progress as a 911 friend.

Experiencing Affirmation in Friendship

Being an **affirming** friend to others means you identify with their good times to increase their joy and identify with their hurt to ease their pain.

Briefly describe how you were an affirming friend to someone recently (perhaps to your friendship partner).

_____

_____

_____

_____

What was the reward or benefit of this experience? How did it help your friend?

_____

_____

_____

_____

If you have not affirmed someone recently, what do you think hindered you?

_____

_____

_____

_____

Experiencing Support in Friendship

Being a **supportive** friend to others means coming alongside them to help lift their load.

Briefly describe how you were a supportive friend to someone recently (perhaps to your friendship partner).

_____

_____

_____

_____

What was the reward or benefit of this experience? How did it help your friend?

_____

_____

_____

Briefly describe how someone (perhaps your friendship partner) was a supportive friend to you and how that helped you.

_____

_____

_____

_____

REMINDER: Be sure to set up a time this week to meet with your friendship partner and talk through Discovery Day Five.

Prayer

Are you satisfied that you are experiencing deepened friendship? Praise God for how He has helped you, and ask Him to help you to pursue being a Christlike 911 friend.

A *911* Friend Is Encouraging

JESSICA'S STORY CONTINUES

Doug Shaw said he was tired of having breakfast alone on Saturday mornings, and that's why he came with Jenny to the pancake house for the last of her three breakfast meetings with Jessica. The three of them laughed at the comment. Actually, Doug came at Jenny's invitation—with Jessica's approval. Doug had also been a source of comfort, support, and encouragement in the month since Jessica's father announced the divorce.

"This was an especially hard week, wasn't it, Jessie?" Jenny said after Doug asked the blessing on the plates of pancakes in front of them.

Jessica nodded. "My parents' divorce was final yesterday. It was kind of a black Friday."

"So how are you doing, Jessie?" Doug asked.

Jessica felt pretty upbeat and tried to sound that way. "Actually, I'm doing OK. I've been hoping and praying all month that my parents would change their minds and get back together. But it didn't happen." Then she added quickly with a smile, "Don't worry: I'm not in denial. I know that Dad and Mom have gone their separate ways. As much as I wish it hadn't happened, I no longer blame myself for it. I still pray that they will find Christ and get back together—in that order."

"That's a good way to pray," Doug assured.

"But yesterday was still a sad day for you?" Jenny probed.

Jessica chewed and swallowed a forkful of Swedish pancake before answering. "Right. I happened to be outside when the postman came by. The official letter was in the stack of mail. I was there when Mom opened it."

"That must have been difficult for you," Jenny said.

Jessica thought for a moment. "Mom seemed relieved that it was all over. I think that bothered me as much as seeing the divorce finalized in black and white. It hurt a little that she was almost glad to be rid of Dad. I guess she doesn't realize that *she* divorced Dad, but *I* didn't. He's still my Dad, and I love him."

Doug put his fork down. "I feel sad for you, Jessie, that your Mom doesn't understand your feelings for your dad."

Jessica rubbed her chin with her thumb. "Thanks, but I'm doing a lot better about things like that. It's like Jenny says, time really helps heal the emotions. I'm able to deal with the hurt a lot better, thanks to our chats during the last three weeks." She flashed a smile of appreciation Jenny's way.

Jenny winked her acknowledgment. Then she said, "How are Karen and Mark doing?"

"Karen still slams a door or two sometimes," Jessica said, "but I think she's getting over it. And Mark seems to be opening up more. I go in and talk to him for a few minutes every night. When I ask how he's feeling, he usually doesn't have much to say. So this week I tried a different approach. I used that list you gave me. I asked him questions, like, 'Mark, do you feel embarrassed about Mom and Dad's divorce? Do you feel sad?' It's a little easier for him to answer yes or no. When he says yes, I try to comfort him and encourage him in that area, like you have done for me."

Jenny beamed. "That's wonderful, Jessie.

You are comforting Mark with the comfort you received." Then she turned to Doug. "I think Jessie is ready to meet Alyson. What do you think?" Doug smiled and nodded.

Jenny turned back to Jessica. "Alyson Gilbert is a new seventh-grader in our middle school group. We found out last week that her parents were divorced in the spring. She moved here with her mother. Doug and I were wondering if you would like to meet Alyson and share your experience with her."

Jessica felt both honored and scared at the same moment. "I don't know about that. I'm not really a counselor. I don't know my Bible that well yet."

"We're not asking you to counsel Alyson," Doug said. "Just share your comfort and encouragement with her as a friend, like you're already doing with Mark. Tell her your story and what you are learning about getting through your parents' divorce. Can you do that?"

Jessica glanced back and forth between Doug and Jenny. "Just do what I'm doing with Mark?" she said. "That's all?" The couple nodded in unison. Suddenly it sounded very simple. "Sure, I can do that," she said confidently. "When can I meet Alyson?"

Doug picked up his fork. "Not until I finish my apple pancakes," he said with a big laugh.

Your 911 Response

Natalie, Doug, and Jenny have been a welcome encouragement to Jessica, and you can see that Jessica's spirits have been lifted. Walk through the following exercises about encouragement with your friendship partner.

Experiencing Encouragement in Friendship

Being an **encouraging** friend to others when they are down means lifting their spirits and helping them focus on the positive and good things in life.

During this Discovery Day, you will take turns sharing the progress each of you has made in becoming a better 911 friend. To prepare, review any of the written comments you made this week about how you are growing as an available, accepting, affirming, and supportive friend to each other and others. As you share, if your friend is dissatisfied with his or her progress in some area, encourage your friend by focusing on positive efforts and outcomes. If nothing else, your friend is still trying, and that's positive!

Work through each of the exercises below together and discuss your progress on each of the friendship qualities. Share your positive reports first. Then talk about any struggles either of you may have in that area. Rejoice with each other and encourage each other. Then journal your responses in the space provided.

Take turns describing to each other your progress at being an **available friend**.

_____

_____

_____

_____

Take turns describing to each other your progress at being an **accepting friend**.

_____

_____

_____

_____

Take turns describing to each other your progress at being an **affirming friend**.

_____

_____

_____

_____

Take turns describing to each other your progress at being a **supportive friend**.

_____

_____

_____

_____

Prayer

Close with a prayer of thanks that God is developing in both of you the qualities that honor Him and make you a trusted, loyal friend who is "born to help in time of need" (Prov. 17:17).

_____

_____

_____

_____

_____

_____

The PROJECT 911 Collection

The story of Jessica in this week's workbook is adapted from the small book entitled *My Friend Is Struggling with Divorce of Parents*. The book is designed as a giveaway book you can read and then give to a friend who has experienced, or is currently experiencing, the separation or divorce of parents. Beyond the fictional story, this book provides practical steps to help a student get through this painful chapter in his or her life.

If you need one or more of these books for a friend, contact your youth group leader. He or she may have a number of copies on hand. If not, this and other books in this collection can be ordered in bulk by calling 1-800-933-9673 ext. 9-2039. Or you may purchase copies of this book at your local Christian bookstore.

WEEK SIX

A 911 Friend Is Accountable

LUKE'S STORY

uke eased up on the accelerator a little, even though he was secretly anxious to get to the top of the hill. But he slowed the car because his girlfriend, Traci, who was seated next to him, was enjoying the view of the city at night on the gently winding road up to the planetarium. And Luke wanted Traci to enjoy the evening because he knew she would make the date more enjoyable for him later if she was happy.

"Look at this, Traci." Luke motioned to the city lights sparkling out his side window. Just as he hoped, Traci leaned toward him as far as her seat belt would allow in order to take in the view. The subtle, sweet fragrance of her hair and skin was delicious. Her left hand touched bare skin at the base of his neck, sending a chill of excitement down his spine. Her right hand rested gently on his thigh. The surge of pleasure tempted him to divert his concentration from the road. But he gripped the wheel determinedly and kept his eyes straight ahead. He didn't want a careless accident to spoil this perfect evening.

"Ooo, it's beautiful, Luke," Traci sang. "Look, you can see the train pulling out of the station down there." Her warm breath brushed his ear, giving him another chill of excitement.

Luke glanced out the window for a half-second. "Yeah, that's neat," he said, even though he never saw the train.

"You're so sweet to bring me up here on such a beautiful night," Traci said. Then she nuzzled him on the cheek with her nose, concluding with a soft peck of a kiss before settling back in her seat. Luke could feel his heartbeat quicken at her closeness. Traci always sparked the greatest feelings in him. He couldn't get enough of her—her looks, her smell, and especially her touch. He was guardedly sure she felt the same way about him.

This had been an expensive evening for Luke. Traci loved romantic dates, so he had treated her to a candlelight dinner at an expensive French restaurant in town. Since it was kind of a dressy evening, he also had to spring for a nice shirt and tie. And the planetarium show at the observatory would cost him another huge chunk of change. As a high-school senior with a part-time job, Luke could hardly afford such a costly date.

But when he picked up Traci at her house tonight, he knew the expense was worthwhile. She looked more like a movie star than a high-school junior in a dress that accentuated her drop-dead figure. She was worth every minute of overtime he would put in next week to replenish his wallet.

"Tell me about the planetarium show at the observatory again," Traci cooed, gently caressing Luke's upper leg. "I can't believe I have lived in town almost a year now and never been up here."

"The planetarium theater has a large, domed ceiling," Luke explained, trying to keep his mind off Traci's hand on his leg. "When the lights are turned off, a special projector fills the dome with specks of light. It looks just like the sky at midnight, full of stars and planets. The narrator points out the major stars and constellations. There are asteroids and shooting stars. It's really cool."

"I love astronomy. I can't wait," Traci said with a cute little laugh. "The stars are so romantic." Luke smiled to himself. As long as Traci felt romantic, he was sure to have a good time.

It was chilly on top of the hill, so Luke wrapped his arm around Traci as they hurried from the parking lot to the planetarium theater. There were at least two hundred people watching the program, Luke figured, but he noticed no one but Traci. She seemed to enjoy the presentation, and Luke enjoyed being close to her, relishing the softness of her hand in his. Encouraged by her closeness, he stole an occasional kiss in the darkness, and Traci responded warmly.

After the show, they strolled to a bench outside where they could see the city lights. Luke draped his jacket around Traci's shoulder and wrapped her in his arms. Huddled with Traci to stay warm, Luke's desire for her heated up. Her willingness spurring him on, Luke's kisses became more intense and passionate than ever before. The pleasure was intense, and he just wanted to be closer to her. Traci's response told him that she wanted the same thing.

Once they returned to the car and resumed their romantic huddling, Luke could hardly keep himself under control. As a Christian, he understood the importance of sexual purity.

He had promised God at youth camp three years earlier that he would remain a virgin until he was married, and he had kept his promise through high school. But his vow had never really been tested until he met Traci Lockhart two months ago. His feelings for her were so strong, not like anything he had felt for other girls. It was a hunger that just seemed to grow more intense with every date.

Swept up in the emotion of the moment, Luke smothered Traci with kisses. Yielding to the urgency he sensed, he touched and caressed her in ways he never had before. Traci seemed so willing, so receptive to the affection Luke yearned to shower on her. It took all the will power he could muster to stop before breaking his promise to God. "We had better get home," he said, pulling away from her reluctantly.

"Yeah, I guess so," Traci said timidly.

They drove home in silence. Luke felt embarrassed for being so bold in his physical approach to Traci, but he seemed almost driven. Why did he feel more strongly toward Traci than any other girl he dated? Why did he feel so compelled to have sex with her? As the car wound down the hill toward the city, the thought occurred to him for the first time: *My desire for Traci is so strong because I must really be in love with her.*

Your 911 Response

Luke thinks he really must be in love, but is he? How can he be sure what he feels is true love? There is the right kind of love and the wrong kind of love. The same is true with friendship. How can we determine the right kind of friendship from the wrong kind of friendship?

The Difference between Right and Wrong Friendship

A lot of people don't know what makes true friendship right. Some claim you can only tell if something is right if it actually works. But if friendship is based on what works for you, what about the following situations? Do you agree or disagree that a true friend would have to do these things to be the right kind of friend? Check (✔) whether you agree or disagree with each statement.

❑ **Agree**   ❑ **Disagree**   "If you are my true friend, you will let me copy your homework assignment because I've been too busy."

❑ **Agree**   ❑ **Disagree**   "If you are really my true girlfriend or boyfriend, you will have sex with me."

❑ **Agree**   ❑ **Disagree**   "If you are my true friend, you will quit being friends with the people I don't like."

Should being a friend to others be based on what is right rather than what a friend might want?   ❑ **Yes**   ❑ **No**

Why?_____

_____

_____

_____

Being an Accountable Friend

Being a true friend doesn't always mean doing what your friend wants you to do, because what he or she may want you to do may not be right. And if it isn't right, it will not be best for you or your friend in the long run.

What is an accountable friend? An accountable friend is a person who can determine right friendship from wrong friendship based on what is absolutely right and wrong. This means that **an accountable friend is answerable to an absolute standard of right and wrong.**

The five qualities of friendship you have been discovering—availability, acceptance, affirmation, support, and encouragement—are actually the absolute standard for right friendships. The reason they work is because they are absolutely right for every situation. In fact, there is something about the rightness of these standards that guarantees they will work to deepen true friendship every time.

How do you feel knowing that availability, acceptance, affirmation, support, and encouragement are guaranteed to work in friendship every time? Check (✔) any words below that apply:

❑ Confident   ❑ Drowsy   ❑ Bloated   ❑ Angry   ❑ Happy   ❑ Secure

Prayer

Thank God today that there is a standard of friendship you can count on. Ask Him to help you to be the right kind of friend, one that others can count on.

_____

_____

_____

_____

_____

A 911 Friend Is Accountable

TRACI'S STORY

Forgive me, God, for compromising my standards, Traci prayed silently as Luke drove her home. She was ashamed about her behavior, seemingly on the verge of breaking her promise to God that she would remain sexually pure. Traci had never intended to go all the way with Luke or any other boy before marriage. But she had been swept away by her emotions tonight. The romantic dinner, the candles, the stars, Luke's eagerness to make her feel special—everything seemed so right. He had been so sweet and affectionate that she would have done anything to please him.

Then, for some reason, Luke stopped before it was too late. Traci was very relieved, but she was also a little disappointed. He was so abrupt that she wondered now if she had done something wrong. *Did he stop because I was too willing? Was I not willing enough? Did I do something that turned him off? Was he disappointed because I didn't measure up to other girls he has been with?* These questions nagged at Traci during the silent ride home. She hoped this would not be their last time together, because she did not want to lose this great guy.

Traci flashed back to their first meeting. It was a weekend ski retreat for the high-school group from the church Luke attended. Traci, who attended a much smaller church across town with a tiny youth group, signed up at the invitation of Polly, a friend from school who attended Luke's church. Traci noticed Luke as soon as she arrived at the church. He

was a leader in the group, welcoming students at the registration table in the parking lot and handing out bus and cabin assignments. Luke was not only nice to her, a first-time visitor; he was nice to everyone, working hard to get the retreat off to a positive start. And he was too cute for words!

Traci was elated when Luke ended up on her bus, sitting only a couple of rows away. During the three-hour drive up the mountain, Traci's attention was divided between chatting with Polly and her friends and secretly watching Luke and his friends, who were having even more fun. Traci admired from a distance Luke's wit and humor, and she was impressed with his respect for the adult leaders and his ability to help everyone have a good time. He led their busload of students in prayer for travel safety and for spiritual and relational growth during the retreat. This was a quality Christian guy, Traci realized, and she wanted to get to know him better.

The weekend afforded so many "unplanned" opportunities to get acquainted that Traci suspected Luke might have noticed her too. He and his friend Curtis showed up at her breakfast table Saturday morning. While Curtis kept Polly occupied, Luke peppered her with questions: How did you find out about our church and the retreat? What is your church like? How long have you been a Christian? How long have you been skiing? What do you plan to do after high school? It was obvious Luke was not like most of the guys she knew. He asked questions about her instead of bragging about himself or trying to impress her with his macho accomplishments. He was interested in her spiritual life. He was courte-

ous, and he actually had table manners. Traci had never before met an eighteen-year-old boy she considered a gentleman. She ate her breakfast slowly because she did not want their first conversation to end.

That afternoon on the slopes, Traci encountered Luke several times. He was a good skier and she was not, so he offered a few helpful pointers without embarrassing her for her limited ability and experience. Luke happened along a few times when Traci fell, helping her up and making sure she was not hurt. And that afternoon in the lodge he appeared with a cup of steaming hot chocolate as she sat by the fire, drying her socks and warming her feet. The strange numbness in her hands flared up again, but she didn't mention it to Luke. They talked for more than an hour, time Luke could have spent skiing. Traci was thrilled. Luke was so kind, so sweet, so polite, and so helpful. She could not believe he was paying attention to her when practically any girl on the mountain would have jumped at the chance to be with him.

Preparing for the Saturday night bus ride home, Traci arranged to leave the seat next to her empty, hoping Luke would sit there when he was finished with the announcements and prayer. He did, and Traci was secretly ecstatic. They talked for three hours, while most of the kids on the bus slept. They shared with each other how they came to Christ, their dreams for the future, and their favorite foods, movies, and music. Traci couldn't believe how much they had in common. Just before they pulled into the church parking lot, Luke asked her out for the next weekend. She accepted immediately, intent on canceling anything on her calendar that might keep her from being with Luke.

The two months from that night to tonight had been magical, Traci assessed. Luke treated her like a princess. Their first date was a picnic by the lake, with Luke fixing the lunch and providing soft music on his boom box. He took her to movies—the romantic kind she liked instead of car-exploding, gun-blazing guy movies. He took her to a play at the performing arts center. They took long walks together downtown and out in the country. They laughed and sang together and even prayed together. On their third date, Luke kissed Traci for the first time, and she lay awake half the night thinking how special she felt to be his girlfriend.

Luke was ever the perfect gentleman—a real-life Prince Charming. He brought flowers to her. He opened doors for her and seated her at tables. He called, and he sent her cards and notes. They kissed and embraced often and held hands most of the time they were together. But Luke had never emphasized the physical side of their relationship—until tonight.

Luke stopped the car in front of Traci's house and, as always, hurried around to her side to open the door. As soon as she stepped out, she was face to face with him in the cool night air. "Traci, I'm . . . I'm sorry about tonight," Luke stammered. "I mean . . . I just . . . felt so close to you. . . . " His voice trailed off, and Traci knew he was having trouble saying what he meant.

"It's all right, Luke," she said reassuringly. "You're so sweet. I know you didn't mean to do anything wrong. I'm glad we stopped. Thank you."

After several silent seconds he said, "Is it OK if I call you tomorrow?"

Traci smiled. "I was hoping you would."

After being kissed lightly on the cheek, Traci went inside. Standing at the window, she watched Luke drive away. *Even tonight he was the perfect gentleman,* she thought dreamily, *apologizing for his passionate advance, asking permission to call me. I forgave him, and I can't wait to talk to him tomorrow. Luke and I have something very special. It must be true love.*

Your 911 Response

Just like Luke, Traci thinks that their relationship must be true love. If what these two are feeling really *is* true love, what makes it true? As with true love, true friendship is true because it conforms to the absolute standard of friendship.

The Friendship Guarantee

What would you think if the standards of friendship—availability, acceptance, affirmation, support, and encouragement—came with a full guarantee to work? What if these qualities are so right that they are guaranteed to deepen friendships every time, for every person, and under every circumstance? In reality, the standards of friendship make this exact guarantee. We are not talking about an approach to friendship that may be right for you but not for someone else. **The 911 standards of friendship are right for everyone.**

911 friendship is also right for any generation of people in any time period. These standards of friendship worked in the first century and they will work just as well in the twenty-first century because they are absolutely right. **The 911 standards of friendship are right for every time period.**

And for this friendship guarantee to work 100 percent of the time, it would have to be right in every situation, no matter how difficult the problem. And they are. **The 911 standards of friendship are right under any and every circumstance.**

This is quite a promise. In order to live up to that promise, the standards of friendship must have three vital characteristics. They will have to be objective, universal, and constant.

Objective

The standards of 911 friendship are objective. What does *objective* mean? Underline the response you believe is correct:

1. It's like when your parents say, "I object to increasing your allowance."
2. When you feel romantic toward someone, you may say, "You are the objective of my affection."
3. Something that exists independently of individual views or opinions.
4. Something to do with parts of speech, because every sentence must have a noun, verb, and objective.

If the standards of friendship are to work for everyone, they must be objective; that is, they must be right totally independent of whether people think they are right or not. In other words, these standards must be absolutely right regardless of a person's view or opinion about them.

Universal

The standards of 911 friendship are universal. What does *universal* mean? Underline the response you believe is correct:

1. Something to do with all the galaxies, planets, and stars.
2. A Hollywood movie company.
3. When everyone likes everyone else.
4. Something that is applied the same everywhere.

If the standards of friendship are to apply in every circumstance and in every culture, they must be universal; that is, they would have to be true everywhere under every circumstance.

Constant

The standards of 911 friendship are constant. What does *constant* mean? Underline the response you believe is correct:

1. An intestinal disorder.
2. Does not change with time.
3. Another word for going steady.
4. The Roman emperor Constantine's uncle.

If the standards of 911 friendship are to be right for any generation in any time period, they must be unchanging, or constant.

How do you feel knowing that a certain kind of friendship is right for everyone, for every time period, under any circumstance? Check (✔) the words that apply.

❑ Assured ❑ Hopeful ❑ Embarrassed ❑ Confident
❑ Secure ❑ Sad ❑ Sleepy ❑ Grateful

There are very good reasons for claiming that the standards of friendship are objective, universal, and constant and therefore absolutely right and guaranteed to work. In Discovery Days Three and Four we will explore those reasons and discover how such a guarantee is possible.

Prayer

Close in prayer by thanking God for the absolute rightness of being an available, accepting, affirming, supportive, and encouraging friend.

_____

_____

_____

_____

_____

_____

_____

A *911* Friend Is Accountable

LUKE'S STORY CONTINUES

uke tugged at the bill of his batting helmet and settled his feet into the batter's box. After a couple of practice swings with the aluminum bat, he called out, "OK, Doug. I'm ready."

Doug Shaw stood outside the batting cage with the coins Luke had given him. At Luke's words, he dropped them into the machine to activate the mechanical pitcher sixty feet from where Luke stood coiled and ready. In a few seconds, it hurled the first baseball toward the center of the strike zone. Luke whipped the bat around to meet it. *Thwang!* The ball shot to the netting high above the mechanical arm and tumbled harmlessly to the cement floor.

"Nice rip, Luke," Doug called out. "It would have been a double deep in the gap, no question." Doug and Luke had just come from a Saturday morning planning breakfast for student leaders in the high-school ministry. As fans of sports in general and baseball in particular, they tried to get to the batting cages once or twice a month together.

After they had worked up a sweat taking cuts in the cage, Doug and Luke bought cans of soda and sat down at a nearby picnic table in the sunshine to drink them. Their conversation was punctuated by the *clink* of baseballs making contact with aluminum bats in the batting cages.

When their discussion of baseball had played out, Doug said, "I notice that you have been spending time with the new girl from Madison High, Traci Lockhart."

Luke studied his can of Dr. Pepper. "Yeah, I have," he said without much expression.

"She seems like a nice girl—very smart, very sweet."

Luke nodded. "Traci is really special," he said.

Doug evaluated the response. "You don't sound very enthused. Is everything all right—I mean, with you and Traci?"

Luke blew a long sigh. "I guess I'm supposed to talk to you about it."

"What do you mean?"

Luke took another drink. "Well, I'm not sure how it's going with Traci and me. I prayed last night that if God wanted me to talk to somebody, you would ask about Traci today. Do you mind if I tell you about our relationship and ask you a few questions?"

"Not at all, Luke," Doug said. "I'm always glad to hear what you have to say, and I'll share what I can."

Luke related his account of meeting Traci during the ski retreat. He explained how he assigned himself to Traci's bus just to be near her, and that he went out of his way to talk to her during the weekend. He described a few of their dates and how close he and Traci had become in just two months. Doug, chuckling, complimented Luke on his ambition and ingenuity. Luke smiled.

Then he quickly sobered. Speaking softly and haltingly, he told about taking Traci to the planetarium last weekend. Omitting the embarrassing details, he summarized how close he came to breaking his vow of sexual purity. He admitted that he was wrong to take advantage of Traci as he did. By the time he finished his story, Luke seemed on the verge of crying.

Discovery Day

"Luke, I can see that your experience last weekend has caused you a lot of anxiety and concern," Doug said. "I feel that with you, my friend, because I love you. And I'm proud of you for doing the right thing in the end." He added an affectionate but manly pat on the shoulder.

"Thanks," Luke said. "I was pretty sure you would understand."

"So where are you and Traci now?" Doug went on. "Did she break up with you?"

"That's the crazy thing about it," Luke returned. "She was glad we didn't . . . you know . . . go all the way. But she's not mad at me or blaming me for what happened. We talked on the phone a couple of times this week, and she wants to keep going out—double dates. We both agreed."

"And how do you feel about Traci after your experience?" Doug said.

Luke brushed a fly away from his ear. "I'm not sure how I feel, Doug. I want to ask you about it."

"Fire away."

"I've never had such strong feelings for a girl before," Luke explained. "I just want to be with Traci all the time. When we are together, I want to touch her and kiss her, and those desires almost got me in big trouble last weekend. Does this mean I'm . . . in love with Traci?"

"The big L-word," Doug said with a slight smile.

"The word *love* never crossed my mind with other girls I've dated," Luke explained. "Traci is different. I just want to know if it really is love."

"How do *you* think a person knows he or she is in love?" Doug asked.

Luke shrugged. "It's some kind of very special feeling, I guess."

"Let me put it another way. What do you think being in love looks like?"

Luke waved at the fly again. "I don't know. Maybe it looks like two people holding hands, going places together . . . "

Doug pulled a slim, leather-bound New Testament from the back pocket of his jeans. "When I first met Jenny in college, I would have answered those questions the same way you did," he said, flipping through pages. "I want to read to you two verses that really helped me understand what true love is." He directed Luke to Ephesians 5:28–29.

Doug found the verses and began to read. "Husbands ought to love their wives as—"

"Whoa, hold on, Doug," Luke interrupted. "We're talking about the L-word here, not the M-word. I'm not a husband, and I don't plan to be one soon. Marriage with Traci is not in my vocabulary, at least not yet. I need to find out if I love her first."

"Relax, buddy," Doug said, laughing, "I'm not trying to herd you to the altar. I just want you to see God's definition of true love. In these verses, love just happens to be applied to husbands and wives. It works in all relationships."

Luke thought for a moment. "Well, OK," he said at last.

Doug started over. "Husbands ought to love their wives as their own bodies. He who loves his wife loves himself. After all, no one ever hated his own body, but he feeds and cares for it, just as Christ does the church."

"I thought Christians were supposed to love others *more* than themselves," Luke said.

"We are to love *God* more than we love ourselves," Doug clarified. "But according to Christ's Great Commandment in Matthew 22, we are to love our *neighbor* as we love *ourselves*. And 'neighbor' includes everyone: parents, brothers and sisters, boyfriend or girlfriend, husband or wife."

"But is it right to love ourselves?" Luke pressed. "I mean, isn't that being kind of self-centered?"

"Paul's not talking about people being selfish or self-centered here," Doug explained. "But we all take care of our own basic needs, like getting enough to eat, getting enough sleep, wearing seat belts and driving carefully, and spending time in the Word to grow. Paul says we should care for the needs of others just as we do for ourselves. In fact, you can tell that love is real when the happiness, health, and spiritual growth of another person is as important to you as your own."

Luke cocked his head. "The way you talk about it, love isn't a feeling at all. Love is a way of treating people—caring for them and being there for them when they need you."

Doug nodded. "Strong feelings of attraction—like you describe between you and Traci—are often called love because that's how it's portrayed in movies, TV, and music.

Good feelings may accompany love, but true love can happen with or without feelings, because love is the activity of caring for a person as you care for yourself."

Luke and Doug talked for another twenty minutes, and Doug led them in a brief prayer. Then Doug left to change clothes and relieve his wife, Jenny, at the quick-print shop. Luke had to leave too, having promised Traci he would take her to buy a battery for her car. Before they parted, Doug issued Luke a specific challenge to apply their discussion in his relationship with Traci. Luke had no idea that Doug's challenge would soon be put to a severe, unexpected test.

Your 911 Response

Doug indicated to Luke that there is a standard that defines true love, just as there is a standard that defines true friendship. Doug quoted Scripture as the standard for love.

Does the Absolute Standard Make It Right?

Where do we get the idea that the standard for true friendship is in being an available, accepting, affirming, supportive, and encouraging friend? We identified these qualities by quoting from one particular source. What was that source? Check (✔) the answer you believe is right:

❑ The Bible
❑ The Boy Scout Handbook
❑ The best-selling book *Green Eggs and Ham*, by Dr. Seuss

Would you agree that the Bible is the true standard of friendship that it is right for everyone, in any time period, and for every circumstance? ❑ **Yes** ❑ **No** ❑ **Not Sure**

Why? _____

_____

_____

_____

If you answered yes to the above question, you are only partially correct. The Bible does communicate the absolute standard of friendship, but the Bible by itself is not what makes a friendship right. If the standard for friendship in the Bible doesn't make friendship right, then what does? Do you have any ideas? Write them here.

_____

_____

_____

Read James 1:17–18:

> "Whatever is good and perfect comes to us from God above, who created all heaven's lights. Unlike them, he never changes or casts shifting shadows. In his goodness he chose to make us his own children by giving us his true word. And we, out of all creation, became his choice possession."

Fill in the blanks in the following statements with answers from the verses above.

Whatever is good and perfect comes from _____.

God never _____.

In God's goodness, He gave us His true _____.

It is the person of God Himself, His character and nature, who is the standard for what is right and perfect and good. While He gave us His Word, and the Bible is true and right, it is only true and right because God is true and right.

God Is the Objective Standard of True Friendship

> "As for God, his way is perfect. All the Lord's promises prove true" (Ps. 18:30).

Fill in the blanks:

God's way is _____ and all His promises prove _____.

The standard of true friendship is objective and right for everyone because that standard comes from God, who is outside us and beyond all of us. Being a caring, available friend is right because the God who created us is by nature a perfect, caring, available friend. He is our refuge (see Ps. 46:1).

God Is the Universal Standard of True Friendship

> "The LORD has made the heavens his throne; from there he rules over everything. Praise the LORD, you angels of his, you mighty creatures who carry out his plans, listening for each of his commands" (Ps. 103:19–20).

Fill in the blanks:

God rules over _____ and the angels carry out His _____ by

listening for each of His _____.

The standard of true friendship is universal and right everywhere, under every circumstance, because that standard comes from someone who rules over everything universally. Accepting others for who they are is right because the very character of God is accepting—He accepted us when we were unacceptable (Rom. 5:6–8).

God Is the Constant Standard of True Friendship

"How can you say the Lord does not see your troubles? How can you say God refuses to hear your case? Have you never heard or understood? Don't you know that the Lord is the everlasting God, the Creator of all the earth? He never grows faint or weary. . . . He gives power to those who are tired and worn out; he offers strength to the weak" (Isa. 40:27–29).

Fill in the blanks:

The Lord who sees your _____ is the _____ God, who never

grows _____ or _____.

He gives power to those who are _____ and _____

_____ and offers strength to the _____.

The standard of true friendship is constant and right for any generation in any time period because that standard comes from someone who is everlasting and unchanging. Affirming others in their joy and sorrow is right because God's very nature is to identify with our joys and to comfort us in our pain (see 2 Cor. 1:3–4). Supporting and encouraging others to help carry their burdens and lift their spirits is right because God Himself is a compassionate God (see 1 Tim. 2:3–6).

Confirm the Meeting Time with Your Friendship Partner

Contact your friendship partner and schedule a time to go over Discovery Day Five together.

_____(day); _____(time);_____(place).

Prayer

Express your thanks to God, who is objective, universal, and constant. Thank Him that the caring, accepting, affirming, supportive, and encouraging heart of true friends originates in God Himself, the absolute standard of true friendship.

A 911 Friend
Is Accountabl

TRACI'S STORY CONTINUES

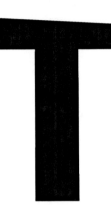

Traci and her mother had cried off and on since their family doctor's phone call earlier that morning. Dr. Duncan did not usually talk to patients on Saturday morning, but today was an exception, he had said. Traci had seen him yesterday about the occasional, bothersome numbness in her hands. She had thought little of the symptoms, but her mother had made an appointment just to check it out. The doctor had deemed it important to call with his preliminary diagnosis.

"Multiple sclerosis?" Traci said to her mother, who had taken the call from the doctor. "I've heard of it, but what is it?"

Jackie Lockhart fought back tears as she explained, "It's a disease of the central nervous system, honey, attacking the brain and spinal cord. They don't know the cause, and they don't know the cure. Depending on the locality of the disease, it can produce . . . disabilities." Jackie could not longer hold back the tears.

"Disabilities? What disabilities?" Traci had demanded, suddenly feeling very afraid. "Mom, what's wrong with me? What's going to happen to me?"

It took Traci's mother several minutes to get through the explanation, interrupted by moments of tears shared with her daughter. Jackie tried to encourage her daughter—and herself—by stating that the symptoms can come and go, disappearing for months or years at a time. But unless a cure was found or

God miraculously intervened, Traci would eventually lose the use of her legs, arms, speech, or other physical abilities. In response to Traci's direct question, Jackie admitted that MS is eventually fatal.

Drying her eyes, Traci went out to the front porch to wait for Luke. It was so sweet and kind of him to help her buy a car battery. In the meantime, Jackie put in a call to her ex-husband to tell him the bad news. Traci's father lived in another state with his second wife.

Sitting on the porch and staring aimlessly, she wondered how Luke would take her news. She had not told him about the numbness in her hands for a couple of reasons. First, until today, the condition was more bother to her than worry, so she didn't think it important to mention. Second, Luke was such a great guy, she wanted to do everything she could to impress him. Volunteering information about her "faults" at this early stage of their relationship was unthinkable.

Now she had to tell him. If she didn't, someone else eventually would, and that would be worse. Besides, it was the right thing to do. As much as she feared that the reality of MS might drive Luke away, the only loving thing to do was to tell him. And she did want to do the loving thing with Luke, because she was pretty sure she loved him. The question plaguing her as she watched for his car was, *Does Luke love me enough to stay with me in spite of what I will tell him?* Behind this question was another she did not want to think about at all: *Does Luke even love me?*

As soon as Luke's car pulled up to the curb, Traci ran to it and jumped in. He noticed her red eyes right away. "You've been crying," Luke said with obvious concern. "Traci, what's wrong?"

Traci blurted out the news along with another wave of warm tears. She felt very ugly crying in front of Luke, but she couldn't help it. It didn't seem to matter anyway. The fact that she was not very pretty when she cried was minor in light of the fact that she might be disabled some day.

Luke's response was more than Traci hoped for. She would not have been surprised had he backed away from her as if she had leprosy, saying something like, "Have a nice life," and left her standing on the curb. After all, a guy as good-looking and sweet as Luke could find a dozen girls without disabilities to go out with by tonight. But instead he touched her

gently and listened intently as she tearfully told her news. He comforted her and encouraged her with caring words. He asked if he could do anything for her. And he promised to stick with her through this tough trial.

Then he helped Traci get her feet on the ground again by taking her to the auto parts store to buy a battery. After installing the battery and giving Traci a tender kiss, he left.

Only later did she begin to wonder if she had seen the last of Luke. Had he been caring, accepting, comforting, and supportive just long enough to make his escape? Was he even now plotting how to escape from this relationship? Or was Luke's concern as genuine as it seemed? Did he know even more about love than what he had shown her in the past two months?

Your 911 Response

How are Luke and Traci going to respond to this difficult turn in their relationship? Whether or not Luke pursues a long-term relationship with Traci that leads to a lifelong commitment, he should commit to the standards of true friendship—availability, acceptance, affirmation, support, and encouragement—in his relationship with her.

We have discovered this week that these standards are absolutely right because they come from an absolute God who is objective, universal, and constant. We also determined that the standards of true 911 friendship are revealed in God's Word, the Bible. "In his goodness he chose to make us his children by giving us his true Word" (James 1:18). God reveals His standard of true friendship for our benefit.

The Purpose of God's Word Revealing His Standards

"All Scripture is inspired by God and is useful to teach us what is true and to make us realize what is wrong in our lives. It straightens us out and teaches us to do what is right. It is God's way of preparing us in every way, fully equipped for every good thing God wants us to do" (2 Tim. 3:16–17).

Underline the phrases in the above verses that explain God's purpose for giving you His Word.

According to 2 Timothy 3, which sentence below best describes God's motivation and heart's desire in giving you His commands and rules for living?

1. God wants to spoil your fun.
2. God wants someone He can boss around.

3. God wanted a best-selling book.

4. God wants to provide for you and protect you.

5. God wants to prove He is right and you are wrong.

Read the following two passages carefully.

"And now, Israel, what does the Lord your God require of you? He requires you to fear him, to live according to his will, to love and worship him with all your heart and soul, and to obey the Lord's commands and laws that I am giving you today for your own good" (Deut. 10:12–13).

"'For I know the plans I have for you,' says the Lord. 'They are plans for good and not for disaster, to give you a future and a hope'" (Jer. 29:11).

Based on the above verses, which statement best illustrates what God's Word, that reflect His standards, does for you? Check (✔) your choice.

❑ It is like **Ann Landers's** newspaper column, read by millions of people daily, that offers advice for people to consider.

❑ It is like a **dictator** who requires absolute obedience.

❑ It is like a **guardrail** that outlines the correct path and provides boundaries to avoid going off the road.

❑ It is like a **coach's playbook** with strategic plays designed to counter the opposing team.

Living Accountable to God's Word

Deuteronomy 10 and Jeremiah 29 tell us that God intends to protect us through the instructions in His Word. His standards for us do provide boundaries. When we cross those boundaries, we suffer the consequences.

But God's Word also provides good things for us as we live in accordance with his instructions. David said in Psalm 119:105, "Your word is a lamp for my feet and a light for my path." That light keeps us from harm and provides us with proper direction.

God knows what really makes friendships work. And His Word provides you with "friendship standards" to help you deepen your friendships. Follow His standards by being a 911 friend, and your friendships will prosper. Be a 911 friend as the Scriptures instruct, and you will experience deepened friendships. Fail to honor these friendship standards, and you will find that the joys and loyalty of friendship will pass you by.

God gave Luke and Traci (and all the rest of us) the command of 1 Thessalonians 4:3, for our benefit as well:

"God wants you to be holy, so you should keep clear of all sexual sin."

How would resisting the pressure of premarital sex benefit Luke and Traci? Check (✔) the statement that you think applies.

❑ They could avoid feelings of guilt.

❑ Luke could avoid being chased out of town by Traci's father.

❑ They could avoid contracting a sexually transmitted disease or Traci getting pregnant.
❑ They could enjoy God's blessing on their relationship.

A 911 friend makes himself or herself accountable to the Word of God. And to help stay accountable, it is a great idea to ask a friend to serve as an accountability partner.

Prayer

Thank God for giving you His Word to provide for you and protect you. Ask Him to help you deepen your commitment to be accountable to His Word.

_____

_____

_____

_____

_____

_____

_____

_____

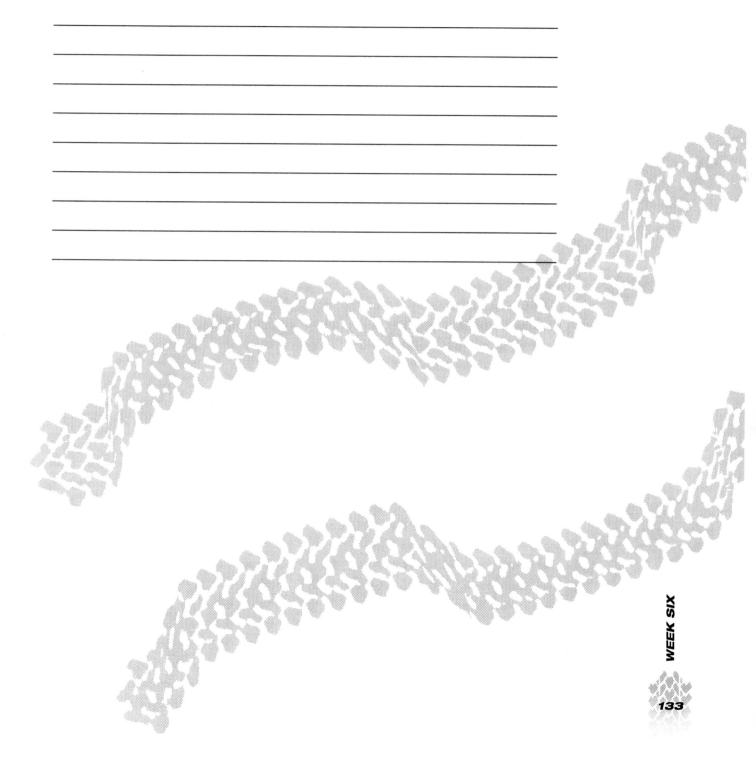

LUKE'S STORY CONTINUES

Discovery Day

Luke sat in his car outside the quick-print shop until almost 6:00 P.M. He approached the door just as Jenny Shaw was coming to lock it and flip the window sign from "OPEN" to "CLOSED." The concern on his face must have been as obvious as a blinking neon sign. "Hi, Luke," Jenny said as he approached the door. "Is something wrong?"

"Can I talk to you and Doug for a minute?" he asked.

"Of course, Luke. Come on in." Jenny locked the door and led him back to the office, where Doug was shutting down a computer.

Luke poured out the story of Traci's recently discovered disease. Doug and Jenny were shocked, saying they would stop by Traci's house on their way home from work.

"I understand a lot more about love since we talked together this morning, Doug," Luke went on. "And I accepted your challenge to begin showing true love to Traci. But I didn't expect this. I mean, Traci is a beautiful girl, but in time her disease could change that. She may not be able to ski or swim or go biking. And if we get married someday—I'm not saying we're going to, but if we do—will she be able to have children? I know true love says 'I love you, period,' but I didn't know that period would be so large."

Both Doug and Jenny put their hands on their young friend. "This has been a tough day for you, Luke," Jenny said, "and we're so sorry about the disappointment you are facing. We will be praying for you as well as for Traci."

"Thanks. That means a lot to me."

Then Doug said, "Only God knows the future, Luke. Only He knows if you and Traci are destined to spend your lives together as husband and wife. That's something you can leave in God's hands, because it's in the future. In the meantime, are you still attracted to Traci, I mean, beyond the physical attraction?"

Luke paused only a moment before answering. "Of course. Traci is a special person. She's fun, smart, happy, and we have so much in common. I admit that her appearance got my attention first. But there is a lot more to Traci than how she looks."

"It sounds like Traci means a lot to you," Jenny put in.

Luke nodded. "Yes, a lot."

"Then you have nothing to lose by making Traci's happiness, health, and spiritual growth as important to you as your own. Loving her God's way will make the most of your relationship right now. And if, in God's plan and timing, you and Traci marry someday, your relationship will be based on true love, not an earthly substitute."

Luke pondered the words for several moments. "OK, but how can I show Traci that I still love her?"

Doug and Jenny spent the next few minutes offering suggestions. When they all stood to leave, Luke hugged and thanked both of them. He told them he was heading back over to Traci's house for a while. The couple said they would see him there after they locked up the store for the night.

Before leaving the shopping center, Luke stopped at the card shop to buy a card for Traci. He selected one he thought she would like, not a mushy, romantic card, but one with a pretty floral design and blank space inside to write.

He wrote only a few quick lines, knowing there would be many other cards, notes, and conversations in the future: "Traci, you are a wonderful person. I know you can get through this. I will be here to help you every step of the way." He rolled the pen in his fingers for several seconds before writing the final two words. They had much more significance to him now, so he wrote them with confidence: "Love, Luke."

Your 911 Response

It's great that Luke has friends like Doug and Jenny to give him advice. But even more, God's Word and the Holy Spirit are there to guide him. As Luke was willing to obey God's Word, he received direction and answers for some tough decisions. As you and your friendship partner make yourselves accountable to God's Word, you too will find clear direction in life.

Walk through the following exercise with your partner.

Accountable to the Word and to Each Other

Second Timothy 3:16–17 says that Scripture teaches us what is true, makes us realize right from wrong, and is God's way of preparing us for the good things God wants us to do.

God's Word is here to guide us, and we should make ourselves accountable to it. Do you find it easy to be accountable to the Scriptures without others helping you? Why? (Write your answer here, and take turns sharing answers with your partner.)

_____

_____

_____

_____

Would you like your friend to lovingly hold you accountable to the standards of friendship so you can be a more available, accepting, affirming, encouraging, and supportive friend to others? If so, how would you like your friend to do that?

_____

_____

_____

_____

Being answerable or accountable to God's Word and having a close friend serve as an accountability partner requires a deep friendship of acceptance. Look back to Week Two, Discovery Day Five where you signed three acceptance pledges. Reaffirm those pledges with each other.

How can your friend encourage you this week and in the weeks to come to continue to be a 911 friend? You might consider asking him or her to pray for you daily, have a regular Bible study with you, review this *Friendship 911 Workbook* with you, etc. Think of one or two things your friend could do to help you in your journey to experience true friendship.

_____

_____

_____

_____

Prayer

Close this time by committing yourselves to each other as friendship partners and thanking God that He is your best friendship partner of all.

_____

_____

_____

_____

_____

_____

_____

_____

The PROJECT 911 Collection

The story of Luke and Traci in this week's workbook is adapted from the small book entitled *My Friend Is Struggling with Finding True Love*. The book is designed as a giveaway book you can read and then give to a friend who wants to know the true standard of love. Beyond the fictional story, this book provides practical steps to discovering what makes love last.

If you need one or more of these books for a friend, contact your youth leader. He or she may have a number of copies on hand. If not, this and other books in this collection can be ordered in bulk by calling 1-800-933-9673 ext. 9-2039. Or you may purchase copies of this book at your local Christian bookstore.

WEEK SEVEN

A **911** *Friend Is An* *Ambassador*

KEN'S STORY

hen his dad walked into his room, fifteen-year-old Ken Meyers knew what he would say. It happened like this at least one evening a week during the school year, sometimes twice.

"I thought you had homework to do," Dad said, lifting the headphones from Ken's ears. Ken bristled inside. He felt like a little kid when his dad just took things away from him like that.

Ken, who had been lying on his bed listening to music, sat up. "I *do* have homework," Ken said, displaying the language-arts worksheet in his hand, "and I'm doing it." He was about halfway through an exercise of diagramming sentences and identifying parts of speech.

"You know you will concentrate better without that noise rattling your brain." Dad motioned toward the headphones.

"It's not noise, Dad, it's music—*Christian* music," Ken said respectfully. He hated the frequent lectures, but it only got worse if he let his attitude get the best of him.

Dad's hands went to his hips, his classic lecture pose. "Kenneth, you need to do better on your grades, and to do that you need to concentrate. I was never able to do homework with

the TV or radio on. It ruins your concentration."

It may ruin your concentration, Dad, Ken thought to himself, *but it doesn't ruin mine. The music actually keeps me relaxed and helps me concentrate. Can't you accept that my study habits may be different from yours?* Ken felt the anger steaming up inside him, but he kept silent.

"You will have to bear down, son, if you want to achieve the grade level that will get you into State University."

I've tried to tell you that I'm not going to State, Dad, Ken argued silently, biting his lip. *In fact, I don't think I want to go to college right away after high school. If you would only listen to me sometime, you might understand what's going on in my life. But all you can think about are my grades.*

Before Ken could object, his dad picked up the CD player and case of CDs from the bedside table. "Let's put this away until your studies are done, OK?" Then he left the room, closing the door behind him.

Ken was so angry he almost cried. If it wasn't his grades or music Dad and Mom disapproved of, it was his clothes or his hairstyle or his friends. And when he wanted to show off his latest Christian CD, his mom and dad were not interested. Ken didn't know which bothered him more: their active disapproval or their passive disinterest. And the fact that his father had ripped off his music made him feel like a prisoner.

Discovery Day

1

Your 911 Response

Conflicts with parents, friends, teachers, and others are inevitable. We know we should avoid conflict whenever possible. Scripture instructs us, "Never pay back evil for evil to anyone. Do things in such a way that everyone can see you are honorable. Do your part to live in peace with everyone, as much as possible" (Rom. 12:17–18). But you can't be around people and totally avoid clashes of opinion, personality, or preferences.

No one really likes conflict, so we need to know how to resolve conflicts and restore friendships on the human level. But some of your friends also need to resolve a longstanding conflict with God and restore a loving relationship with Him. So we also must know our role as a 911 friend in helping to resolve that conflict. A key word for understanding our role is *ambassador*.

What Is an Ambassador?

The Bible says,

> "God . . . reconciled us to himself through Christ and gave us the ministry of reconciliation: that God was reconciling the world to himself in Christ . . . And he has committed to us the message of reconciliation. We are therefore Christ's ambassadors, as though God were making his appeal through us" (2 Cor. 5:18–20 NIV).

First, what does *reconcile* mean? Check (✔) the statement that you think defines *reconcile*.

❑ When you think something is true, like saying, "I reckon so."
❑ When you reuse valuable materials, like reconciling aluminum cans.
❑ When you restore a friendship between two persons in conflict.

To reconcile means to resolve a conflict or restore people to friendship. As the verses above state, God has given each of us His message so people can be restored to friendship with God. We are called God's ambassadors for sharing that message.

So what is an ambassador? Check (✔) the statement that you think best describes an ambassador.

❑ A breed of medium-sized hunting dogs.
❑ An authorized messenger or representative.
❑ A chain of large hotels.

An ambassador is an authorized messenger or representative. In government, an ambassador is appointed by one country to represent it in another country, such as the United States ambassadors to France, Japan, South Africa, etc. An ambassador takes the message of his or her country to another country. As God's ambassadors, we are His authorized messengers or representatives to tell others that they can be restored to friendship with God.

But as God's messenger, what if *you* have unresolved conflicts with others, such as a parent or friend? Can those conflicts hinder you from being a good ambassador for Christ? Why?

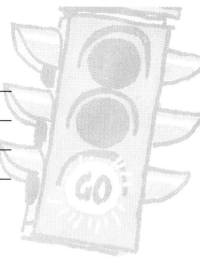

_____

_____

_____

_____

"We try to live in such a way that no one will be hindered from finding the Lord by the way we act, and so no one can find fault with our ministry" (2 Cor. 6:3).

Check (✔) the statement that applies. "One of the most important things you can do to be a good witness and messenger for God is to . . .

❑ . . . make a lot of money so people will want what you have."
❑ . . . love one another so they will know you are a follower of Christ."
❑ . . . spend the rest of your life alone in a cave praying for the return of Christ."

Fill in the blanks from the following verses:

Just as I have _____ you, you should _____ each other. Your love for

one another will _____ to the world that you are my _____.

"Just as I have loved you, you should love each other. Your love for one another will prove to the world that you are my disciples" (John 13:34–35).

Whenever you are an available, accepting, affirming, encouraging, and supportive friend to others, you actually advertise that you are a disciple of Christ. The love and friendship you show others communicates clearly that you are God's ambassador and a good witness for Christ. How do you feel about being a walking advertisement for Christ?

_____

_____

_____

_____

Prayer

Close by asking God to deepen your friendships with others in your youth group so you can be a better witness for Him.

_____

_____

_____

_____

_____

A *911* Friend Is An Ambassador

KEN'S STORY CONTINUES

Discovery Day

2

Just before 10:00, Ken climbed into bed for the night. He had not finished his homework. Tonight's clash with his dad had sapped him of the little motivation he had. He knew another incomplete assignment would pull down his grades even further. But what difference did it make? Even if he notched a 4.0 for the semester, he figured his parents would continue to chip away at his other differences and failures. For all his efforts, he couldn't seem to win with them. So why try?

Lying in the darkness, Ken lifted a silent prayer. *God, I know You love me, but why are Dad and Mom so against me? Why don't they care about me anymore? I know some things I do really tick them off. But they seem to hate everything about me. It's like they are tired of being my parents and would just rather I grow up and move out. God, what can I do?*

As Ken prayed, it occurred to him that home wasn't the only place where his relationships were wearing thin. The face of Todd Wallace, his friend at church, suddenly popped into his mind. *Yeah, some friend,* Ken thought cynically. *Todd is great to be around when we're doing what he wants to do. But when I ask him to go the sports-card shop with me or need his help on the youth group outreach event, he is suddenly "too busy." It's like he's my friend when I fit in with his plans or when he needs something. Otherwise he couldn't care less.* Ken quickly added a postscript to his prayer. *And, God, why can't Todd and I be true friends?*

Just before drifting off to sleep, Ken thought about Doug Shaw. A year earlier, Doug had really helped Ken make the transition from getting by on his parents' faith to trusting Christ personally for himself. Ken loved the youth group at church, and he considered Doug to be kind of a spiritual big brother. Doug Shaw frequently told students in the group that he and Jenny were available to talk with them about anything. For the first time since he had met Doug, Ken realized he had something to talk about with his "big brother."

After school the next day, Ken walked to the small quick-print shop Doug and Jenny owned and operated. The shop was not exactly on Ken's way home, but he walked the extra six blocks anyway, hoping Doug was there and had a few minutes to talk.

Walking into the shop, Ken felt a little odd. He had never done anything like this before. Should he have made an appointment? What was he supposed to say? "Hey Doug, I have a problem. Will you stop working and solve something for me?" That didn't seem to sound too good. As it turned out, Ken didn't have to worry about it. Doug, who was doing layout on one of the shop's computers, saw him come in the door.

"Hi, Ken," he said cheerfully. "What a nice surprise to have you drop in." Jenny, who was waiting on a customer at the counter, also waved and smiled. Ken waved back. "Give me a couple of minutes, Ken," Doug called over the counter, "and I'll take a break. There's something I want to tell you. We can get something to drink."

"Sure," Ken said, nodding. Doug made him

feel like a welcomed guest instead of an interruption in his schedule. It was a feeling he had been missing at home, where he sometimes felt like an intruder or a pest.

Five minutes later, Doug and Ken left the shop in Jenny's care and headed down the sidewalk toward a health-food shop called The Blender. As they walked, Doug grabbed Ken by the shoulder and gave it a gentle squeeze. "I want to thank you for helping out with the sound during our youth outreach event last weekend," Doug said. "I saw you toting mike cords and speakers all over the place, and I appreciate your help."

Ken enjoyed getting caught doing something good for a change. He had worked hard with the sound crew during the big event, and he didn't think anybody noticed. "I enjoyed it," he said. "I would like to work with sound again sometime."

They both bought a cold fruit smoothie and sat down at a booth to drink them. They talked about the great music and dynamic speaker at the youth outreach event and the number of students who trusted Christ as their Savior that night. Ken knew Doug had to get back to the shop soon. It would have been easy to skip the real reason he had come to see Doug. But he was afraid things would get much worse at home if he didn't talk to someone soon.

Your 911 Response

Ken has some unresolved conflicts that are robbing him of the joy of living and hindering him from being a good ambassador of God's love for others. If you and I are not living up to the standards of friendship, we are hindering God's message from being effectively communicated through us, plus we are reflecting badly on Christ, the One we represent.

How Conflict Hurts All of Us

Seventeenth-century English poet John Donne wrote these familiar words: "No man is an island, entire of itself; every man is a piece of the Continent, a part of the main." What do you think he meant? Check (✔) the statement that makes the most sense to you:

❏ Nobody should live in Hawaii because it's too far from the mainland.
❏ We are all connected to each other in some way, and we need each other.
❏ The next time you attend a Halloween party, don't dress up as an island.
❏ You can see reruns of *Gilligan's Island* all over the continent.

Mr. Donne wasn't the first person to realize that we are all connected and need each other. The apostle Paul wrote:

"The human body has many parts, but the many parts make up only one body. So it is with the body of Christ" (1 Cor. 12:12).

First Corinthians 12 teaches that Christians are a part of Christ's body. Just like the human body, Christ's body has many different parts but they all fit together to form one body.

Below are listed several parts of the human body. Check (✔) the one that you think is the most important.

❑ eyes   ❑ nose   ❑ hands   ❑ ears   ❑ heart   ❑ feet

Did you choose the heart as the most important?   ❑ **Yes**   ❑ **No**

What if the other parts of the body got really ticked off because you did not choose them as most important? What if they decided to say, "I'm out of here" in protest? What would you lose? Complete each statement below.

✳ If my eyes said, "We quit," I would lose my _____.
✳ If my ears said, "Good-bye," I would lose my _____.
✳ If my nose said, "I'm leaving," I would lose my sense of _____.
✳ If my feet said, "We're out of here," I would lose my ability to _____.

Your nose may not be as important as your heart, but it is still a necessary part of your body. All your body parts need to stay together and work together for the body to function properly. In the same way, you need every other person in your youth group for your group to really be honoring to God. When you are in unity with each other, you can be good ambassadors for God.

Paul goes on to say in 1 Corinthians 12:

"Yes, there are many parts, but only one body. The eye can never say to the hand, 'I don't need you.' The head can't say to the feet, 'I don't need you.' . . . This makes for harmony among the members, so that all the members care for each other equally. If one part suffers, all the parts suffer with it, and if one part is honored, all the parts are glad" (vv. 20–21, 25–26).

In what way might each of us suffer if there is division and conflict in the body of Christ? If you have a conflict with your parents or another student, how does it affect your witness for Christ? Does a conflict also cause you to suffer? How?

_____

_____

_____

A conflict between you and a parent or friend may mean that person is not there for you when you need him or her. In the following scenarios, what needed quality of friendship might you miss out on if an unresolved conflict separates you from someone? Fill in the missing words from the list below.

Support   Comfort   Encouragement   Available

If I suffer a major disappointment, conflict may keep my parent or friend from providing the _____ I need to ease my pain.

If I get behind on my studies, conflict may keep my parent or friend from offering the _____ I need to lighten my load.

If I feel rejected by my teammates for missing a big game, conflict may keep my parent or friend from sharing the _____ I need to lift my spirits.

If I am struggling with a problem, conflict may keep my parent or friend from being _____ to care, listen, and be a safe zone.

We must resolve our conflicts with one another and pursue unity in order to be true 911 friends and ambassadors of God's love to the world.

Prayer

Close by thanking God that He has made each of us part of His body. Ask Him to help you develop greater oneness with family members and friends.

_____

_____

_____

_____

_____

_____

_____

_____

Discovery Day

3

have kind of a prayer request to talk to you about, if you don't mind," Ken said, fiddling with the straw in his drink.

"I don't mind at all, Ken," Doug assured. "What can I pray with you about?"

Ken had told no one but God what he was about to reveal to Doug. The thought of actually telling another person about the anger and hurt he felt toward his parents and his friend Todd made him pause to swallow a surprising lump of emotion that had suddenly crept into his throat. "I'm . . . I'm having trouble with my parents. We're not getting along very well right now." He briefly described the latest clash with his dad over the CD player. "It seems that everything I do is stupid or wrong. They're always ragging on me about my clothes or my music or my grades. They don't seem to care about who I am and what I like. Sometimes I feel like I'm living in the house alone. I don't know if they really love me." When he finished his explanation, Ken was fighting back his emotions.

Doug's face clouded with sadness. "Ken, I can see that this really hurts you. I'm sorry you doubt your parents' love. Seeing you in pain like this really hurts me."

Ken felt some of the weight lift from him. Just knowing that Doug understood where he was coming from and hurt for him was a measure of relief he had not expected. Feeling his confidence swell, Ken went on to tell Doug about his recent difficulties in getting along with Todd Wallace.

After a few respectful moments, Doug said, "Tell me more about your relationship with your parents and Todd."

"What do you want to know?"

Doug asked several questions about Ken's relationship with his parents. Then he gently probed into Ken's friendship with Todd. Each sad answer was accompanied by a shadow of sorrow on Doug's face.

Finally Doug said, "I have to get back to the shop. But maybe we can get together again soon when we can talk more about the conflicts in your relationships and pray together. Would that be OK?"

"Yeah, that would be OK."

Since they both attended the 9:30 A.M. worship service on Sundays, they decided to meet at church during the 11:00 A.M. service. Doug said he knew about an empty Sunday-school classroom they could use. Ken eagerly agreed.

"Until then," Doug said, "I want you to know that I care about you, Ken. I know it hurts to feel that your parents don't understand you and that Todd is so self-centered in his friendship with you. I want to stay with you though this. I'll be praying for you. In fact, let me say a prayer for you right now." Ken felt a lump in his throat as Doug quietly asked God to share His comfort with Ken.

When Doug said good-bye and returned to the shop, Ken was not eager to go home. He knew he would probably be quizzed and criticized for getting home late. And he sure couldn't tell Todd about his talk with Doug. But he felt a spark of comfort and encouragement knowing that he was not alone in his pain. Doug knew and Doug cared, and that meant a lot to Ken. It gave him a glimmer of hope that his relationships with his dad and Todd might someday be better.

Your 911 Response

Ken's conflicts are hindering him, his dad, and Todd from being the kind of friends they need to be to each other. But this conflict also hinders them from being effective ambassadors of God's message to others around them.

The World Is Watching

Jesus prayed to his heavenly Father:

> "My prayer for all of them is that they will be one, just as you and I are one, Father . . . so they will be in us, and the world will believe you sent me" (John 17:21).

Jesus prayed that we would be in unity with each other ("That they will be one"). When we are in harmony with each other and are one with Christ and the Father, what will result?

"The world will _____."

Why will the world believe that God sent Christ simply by seeing Christians in unity with God and loving each other? Check (✔) the appropriate answer.

❑ Love makes the world go around.   ❑ Love is blind.
❑ Love makes people think straight.   ❑ Love in action draws people to God.

Jesus prayed to His Father:

> "I have given them the glory you gave me, so that they may be one, as we are—I in them and you in me, all being perfected into one. Then the world will know that you sent me and will understand that you love them as much as you love me" (John 17:22–23).

Fill in the blanks from the verses above.

"The world will know that you sent me and will _____ that you

_____ them as much as you love me."

> "I have loved you, my people, with an everlasting love. With unfailing love I have drawn you to myself" (Jer. 31:3).

What is it that draws people to God? _____.

God uses His love in action to draw people to Himself and persuade them that He loves them and wants friendship with them.

Ambassador: God Loving through You

As God's ambassador, you are His messenger to tell people about His love. But there is much more to your special role. God actually loves others through your life! The Bible tells us that our

love for others comes from God, and "if we love each other, God lives in us, and his love has been brought to full expression through us" (1 John 4:12).

When you are accepting in loving friendship to someone, where does that acceptance originally come from? Check (✔) the answer you choose.

❑ From my big heart   ❑ From God

❑ From www.acceptance.com   ❑ From reading love stories

When someone receives acceptance or comfort or support from you in a friendship, who is that person actually receiving it from? Check (✔) the answer that applies.

❑ From God only

❑ From me only

❑ From God through me

❑ The apostle Paul said:

"We loved you so much that we gave you not only God's Good News but our own lives, too" (1 Thess. 2:8).

When you are a 911 friend to someone by the power of God's love, you are His ambassador. God is sharing His love through your life! The loving acceptance, affirmation, availability, comfort, and encouragement you give come from God. Yet He is pleased to channel His love through your friendship with others. How does that make you feel?

❑ Tired   ❑ Forgetful   ❑ Involved in God's ministry of love

❑ Significant   ❑ Helpful   ❑ Like I have purpose

Confirm the Meeting Time with Your Friendship Partner

Contact your friendship partner and schedule a time to go over Discovery Day Five together.

_____(day);_____(time); _____(place).

Prayer

Thank God that He involves you as His ambassador and shares His love with others through you.

_____

_____

_____

_____

_____

_____

A 911 Friend Is An Ambassador

KEN'S STORY CONTINUES

Ken's mind often wandered during the sermon, but it was especially difficult paying attention today. Sitting with his parents and his sister, Hillary, in the sanctuary, Ken considered the irony. To others in the church, the Meyerses probably looked like the ideal Christian family. But to Ken, this didn't feel like a family at all. His parents seemed more like jailers, restricting his privileges and general enjoyment of life until he had served his "sentence" and earned his freedom at age eighteen. Ken wondered if anything Doug Shaw could say would make a difference in his relationship with Dad and Mom. He had similar doubts about his friend Todd.

A little after 11:00, Ken met Doug in an empty Sunday-school classroom. Ken had not told his parents *why* he was meeting with Doug, only that Doug wanted to talk to him. Dad and Mom eagerly gave permission for Ken to stay, saying they would pick him up in front of the church at noon. *They probably hope Doug will talk some sense into me,* he thought cynically.

"How's it been going at home since we talked last week, Ken?" Doug began.

Ken shrugged. "About the same, I guess. It's like I'm not even part of the family. I live there and sleep there, but Dad and Mom don't notice me unless I do something they don't like—and they seem to find plenty of those things each week."

"I'm sorry that you don't feel as close to your parents as you want to," Doug said. "I've been praying for you since we talked at The Blender."

Ken dropped his head sheepishly. "Thanks." Doug's prayers and concern meant more to him than he could express. "And thanks for the note you sent to me. It really helped."

"Let me ask you a question, Ken," Doug continued. "It will help us get into your struggles with your parents. And it will lead us to some guidelines that will help you at home and with your friend Todd."

Ken nodded. "OK, shoot."

"Have you ever said something like this at home: 'Hey, Mom and Dad, I'm getting hungry. What's for dinner?'"

Ken raised an eyebrow, wondering where Doug was going with his question. "Of course, like about five times a week. What do you mean by—"

Doug cut him off with his next question. "And do your parents always provide dinner and other meals for you?"

"Yeah, sure," Ken said, still wondering what food had to do with his problem. "And if they aren't around at mealtime, there is always something in the fridge I can nuke. Why?"

"Let me ask one more question, then I think you will understand," Doug said. "Have you ever said to your mom or dad, 'I'm really feeling ignored. Do you have fifteen minutes you can spend with me?'"

Ken studied Doug's expression, which conveyed that he had a secret he was just bursting to tell. "No way," Ken answered finally. "I mean, can you imagine any kid like me saying that to his parents? It never happens."

Discovery Day

4

Doug pressed on. "But when you're hungry, you're not afraid to ask them for something to eat, right?"

"Right."

"Then why can't you tell them about your other needs and allow them to meet them?"

Ken didn't answer because he didn't know what to say. He had never considered telling his parents what he really felt.

Apparently Doug wasn't expecting an answer, because he kept talking. "From what you have told me, Ken, your relationship with your parents would probably improve if they just sat down and listened to you occasionally and showed a little interest in some of your activities."

Ken smiled at the incredible thought. "It sure couldn't hurt."

"And how would you feel if they started noticing your positive behavior and complimenting you when you did something right?"

Ken gave a small laugh. "I'd feel like they were on drugs."

Doug grinned at the humor. Then he said, "Seriously, if your parents began treating you this way, would your relationship begin to change? Would you sense that they were better expressing their love to you?"

Ken didn't hesitate. "Of course, but—"

Doug interrupted him by holding up his hand like a stop sign. "How will your parents understand how you want to be treated unless you tell them?" He didn't wait for an answer. "You have certain relational needs, Ken—everybody does. You tell Mom and Dad about your physical hunger for food, and they fill that need. I believe if you tell them about your relational hunger for their attention and acceptance, they will try to meet those needs too, because I think they really do love you."

Ken felt a mild flash of panic. "What do you mean by 'tell them'?"

"I mean 'tell them,'" Doug explained with an impish smile. "You sit down with your par-

ents, explain your needs, and give them an opportunity to meet them. The same is true for Todd. You need to let him know the kind of friend you want to be to him and how you would like that kind of friendship in return."

Ken was on his feet and pacing. "I don't know if I can do that with my parents," he said nervously.

"Sure you can," Doug said, sounding rock-solid confident. "I'll even go with you if you want."

Ken stopped pacing. "You'll talk to my parents for me?"

"I'll talk to your parents *with* you," Doug corrected, "after you and I have talked and prayed together about your specific needs and how they can be better met."

Ken could hardly believe it. "You would really do this?"

"Sure I would," Doug said. "And once we have gone through the process with your parents, you will know how to talk to Todd."

"That would be great," Ken said, dropping back into his chair with a relieved sigh.

During the next forty minutes, Doug helped Ken think through and list on paper specific areas where his relationship with his parents was strained. The discussion helped them identify some of Ken's relational needs that could use some attention at home. Then they prayed together that God would prepare the way for a positive, productive meeting with Ken's parents. Doug suggested that they repeat the process with Todd after Ken cleared the air with his mom and dad.

When Ken's dad arrived to pick him up, Doug asked if he could stop by later in the afternoon for a visit. "Ken and I have something we want to share with you," he said cordially. Mr. Meyers agreed. Ken rode home in silence, already nervous about the meeting but also hoping that something good was about to happen between him and his mom and dad.

Your 911 Response

Ken is about to discover that being honest in his relationships can be positive. But he should not pin his hopes and expectations for having his needs met on his parents or Todd. While God is pleased to love Ken through his parents and friends, Ken needs to place his trust first in God to meet his needs. God never fails, but Ken's parents or friends will fail at times to be God's channel to meet his relational needs. If Ken is counting on them alone, he will feel let down and discouraged.

As a 911 friend, you can be God's channel of love to your friends, even when they are struggling with conflicts with parents or others.

God Is Looking for a Few Good Ambassadors

Doug Shaw has become an ambassador of friendship to Ken. Ken was missing some things in his relationship with his parents and with Todd. What did Ken need relationally? Check (✔) the boxes that apply.

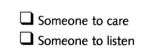

- ❑ Better grades
- ❑ Some encouragement
- ❑ Stricter rules
- ❑ Someone to support him
- ❑ Someone to care
- ❑ Someone to listen

Other than your friendship partner, are there students around you who need someone to care about them, to listen to them, and to be a safe zone for them? Do you see students who need to feel accepted for who they are, regardless of what they have done? There are those who need to be affirmed in their joys and comforted in their troubles. Others may need support to lift their burdens or encouragement to lift their spirits.

God is looking for a few good ambassadors through whom He desires to make His appeal of love to students in need of a friend (see 2 Cor. 5:21). God wants to involve you in His ministry of reconciliation—restoring to friendship. God is pleased to draw students to Himself by loving them through you as a 911 friend.

God Is a 911 Friend

God wants you to be His messenger to others, letting them see and experience what kind of friend God can be to them. Obviously, God doesn't need you to be His channel of love. He is God, and He can and does get involved directly in the lives of the people you know, completely apart from what you do. God is the perfect 911 friend, even when you are not involved. But He also wants to involve you in ministering His love to your friends. God wants to be a 911 friend to your friends through you.

God Is an Available and Accepting Friend through You

How has God chosen to demonstrate some of His acceptance and available friendship to those around you? Check (✔) the answer that seems correct.

- ❑ He gives through the United Way.
- ❑ He is no longer accepting and available because He has gone back to heaven.
- ❑ God advertises His availability and acceptance on the Internet.
- ❑ God demonstrates some of His availability and acceptance through us when we are accepting and available to our friends.

Jesus said:

> "The words I say are not my own, but my Father who lives in me does his work through me . . . The truth is, anyone who believes in me will do the same works I have done, and even greater works, because I am going to be with the Father" (John 14:10, 12).

God the Father lived in Christ and worked and loved through Him. Who does Christ want to live and love through now?_____

God Is an Affirming, Encouraging, and Supportive Friend through You

How has God chosen to demonstrate His affirming, encouraging, and supportive friendship? Check (✔) the answer you believe is correct.

- ❑ He has given us beautiful music to make us feel better.
- ❑ His beautiful creation provides everything we need.
- ❑ God demonstrates some of His affirmation, encouragement, and support through you when you are affirming, encouraging, and supportive to your friends.
- ❑ God expects us to make it on our own.

Jesus said to His disciples:

> "And I will ask the Father, and he will give you another Counselor, who will never leave you. He is the Holy Spirit, who leads into all truth. The world at large cannot receive him, because it isn't looking for him and doesn't recognize him. But you do, because he lives with you now and later will be in you" (John 14:16–17).

Who do you think God wants to reveal Himself through to help your non-Christian friends recognize that He is an available, accepting, affirming, supportive, and encouraging friend? _____

Jesus may not be here in His own body to be an available, accepting, affirming, supportive, and encouraging friend to those around you. But you are His ambassador. His human body may not be visible, but His Spirit is here. He wants to live and love through you by the power of His Holy Spirit.

Will you submit your heart, mind, and body to God's Holy Spirit? As you do, He will empower you to share His love and friendship, and fellow students will recognize it is Christ in you!

Can You Explain Your Hope?

God has a plan for you—"plans for good and not for disaster, to give you a future and a hope" (Jer. 29:11).

We have discovered that God wants to restore the friendship with His human creation that He once enjoyed with Adam and Eve before sin entered the world. He wants to restore the friendship with every person who does not know Him. Jesus Christ is the only hope for that to happen. You are God's ambassador to share that message. He wants you to give your friendship to others so that they will recognize Christ in you, because Christ is their only hope of restored friendship with God.

The apostle Peter writes:

"You must worship Christ as Lord of your life. And if you are asked about your Christian hope, always be ready to explain it" (1 Pet. 3:15).

This *Friendship 911 Workbook* has helped you become a channel of God's friendship to others. But as God's ambassador, you also need to be able to explain your hope of salvation in Christ to others.

Do you feel that you can clearly explain to your non-Christian friends why Christ is their only hope for salvation? Can you explain it in such a way that they will be attracted to Christ?

❏ **Yes**   ❏ **No**   ❏ **I could use some help explaining it.**

By living out your hope in Christ and being able to explain your hope in Christ, you will be a powerful ambassador for God.

NOTE: *Other books, videos, and workbooks from Josh McDowell's Beyond Belief campaign will soon be available to help you learn to better explain your hope to others. Ask your youth leader about them.*

Prayer

Offer yourself to God as His ambassador. Tell Him you want your nonbelieving friends to see Him in you and hear His message through you. Tell God you want to more effectively live out and explain that Christ is the only hope for every student. Thank Him for the privilege of being His ambassador.

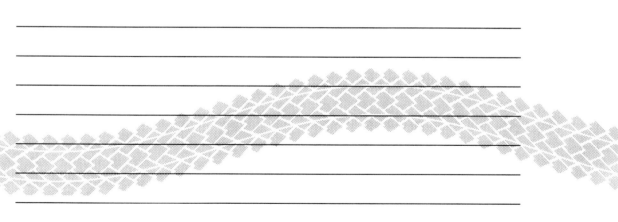

Mom and Dad, I've been talking to Doug recently, and he has really helped me see some things in my life more clearly." Ken was so nervous that his voice squeaked when he spoke. He couldn't help it. It was late Sunday afternoon, and he was seated with his parents in the family room of their home. Doug Shaw was sitting nearby. Ken's younger sister was at a friend's house for the afternoon.

Ken went on. "As we talked, I understand more that you have really taken good care of me. I mean, you've given me a nice home and plenty to eat. You buy most of my clothes and stuff for me. I just want you to know that I'm thankful for all that. I know I don't tell you that enough." Ken swallowed hard. "And I . . . I love you both."

He noticed a glimmer of a smile on their faces. "We love you too, Kenneth," his mom said. Dad nodded.

Ken cleared his throat. He found it very difficult to say these words, and he wished he could leave the room and let Doug do the talking for him. But he knew he had to go on.

"Since you are so good at taking care of me and all I . . . I want to tell you about a couple other areas where I kind of need your help. OK?"

"Of course, Ken," Dad said. Both his parents waited expectantly.

Ken squirmed uncomfortably in his seat, glanced at Doug for encouragement, then began. "Well, I'm learning that I have a pretty big need for your acceptance. I know I mess up a lot, and you tell me about it when I do. I need to be corrected sometimes. But it would help if I thought you noticed some things I did were OK too. Maybe if you saw me doing something right, you could let me know or something."

Ken was too nervous to look his parents in the eye. He stole a glance at Doug, who flashed him a "good-job" smile. Then he waited.

After several silent seconds, his dad asked, "Do you really think we don't accept you?"

"Sometimes, Dad, especially when I only hear that my grades aren't good enough, that you don't like my clothes, that my room is always messy . . . " Ken could have added more to the list, but he didn't want to overdo it.

"Kenneth, you're our son," his dad said, "and we're very proud of you. We only point out those things because we want the best for you."

Ken nodded. "I know, Dad. But when all I hear about is what needs to change, I sorta get discouraged. It's like the other night, when you took away my CD player. I was working on my homework, and it was half done. But you didn't see that. Instead, all I heard about was how bad my music and study habits were. And I end up thinking you don't really like me that much."

Doug cut in respectfully. "Ken, maybe it would help if you would tell your dad what you would like to hear him say in a situation like the other night."

Ken thought for a moment. Then, turning toward his dad, he said, "It would really help if you said something like, 'How is your homework going?' And when I showed you my

Discovery Day

worksheet, you might say, 'You're doing OK so far. If you need any help, ask me. Just don't let the music distract you.'"

Feeling more confident, Ken watched Dad process his comment. After several moments, his father began to nod. "I think I see what you mean, son. I didn't realize I was so one-sided. I'm sorry I was so hard on you the other night, and at other times too. I guess I am so eager for you to succeed that I forget to notice when you *do* succeed. I do love you, son, no matter if your grades are good or not. I'm very sorry I haven't told you that."

Before Ken could respond, his mother apologized for not being more accepting and asked his forgiveness. When Ken verbalized his forgiveness, Mom said, "We will do our best to notice your strengths and let you know we love you even if you don't always measure up."

Greatly encouraged by his parents' positive response, Ken went on to his second big need: for their availability. He explained the loneliness and frustration he felt when they didn't listen to him, spend time with him, or show an interest in his activities. "It would be great sometimes," he concluded, "if you could just come into my room, ask how I'm doing, and listen to me." His parents apologized again and promised to be more available.

Ken was prepared to stop there. He could hardly believe his parents' positive response to his words, and he didn't want to overburden them with his feelings. But Mom said, "This is very helpful to us, Kenneth. We didn't know how hurt you were feeling. Is there anything else?"

Ken and his parents went on to discuss a few other issues. Eventually his mother stood up and approached her son with a hug.

Standing to meet her, Ken received his mom's warm embrace. In seconds Dad was there too, and they all held each other until the three of them were fighting back tears. Then Doug Shaw joined in and prayed a short prayer for the Meyers family.

"There's just one thing," Ken said, wiping his face with the back of his hand. There was a smile of mischief on his face. "I don't mind the hugs, but not when my friends are around, OK?" The four of them enjoyed a good, long laugh.

A few minutes later, when Doug explained that he had to leave, Ken walked him to the front door. "Thanks, Doug, thanks a lot for . . . you know . . . just, thanks."

"No problem, Ken," Doug returned. "I think it turned out well. You did a great job, and your parents . . . well, I think they really love you."

Ken grinned and nodded.

Doug opened the door and stepped out on the porch, then he turned to face his young friend. "Are you feeling OK about talking to Todd? Do you want me to go with you?"

Ken thought for a moment. "Thanks for offering, Doug, but I'll be OK. Talking to my folks today really helped me see how I need to talk to Todd. I think I can do it by myself . . . except for your prayers, of course."

"I know you can do it, Ken," Doug affirmed as he stepped off the porch, "and I will be praying for you. Just let me know how it turns out." Then he waved and turned toward his car.

"Will do," Ken called after him. Closing the door, he was almost excited about clearing the air with his friend Todd.

Your 911 Response

Ken reconciled—restored a friendship—with his parents, and he is about to do the same with Todd. But it was his caring friend Doug who helped him understand what availability and acceptance really meant. As Doug became God's ambassador of availability and acceptance, Ken found the understanding and courage to let his parents know he needed them too.

Walk through the following exercises with your friendship partner.

Spreading 911 Friendship

Do you need to resolve any conflicts with others, or do you know of others who want to resolve conflicts with their friends? Take turns sharing your responses with each other.

_____

_____

If there is a conflict you need to resolve, or if you have a friend who wants to resolve conflicts, get the booklet, *My Friend Is Struggling with Conflicts with Others* from your youth leader. It explains in detail how to resolve conflicts according to God's plan. For more information on this book, see the explanation at the end of this Discovery Day.

Describe one or two of your most significant experiences during these weeks about friendship. Take turns relating them to each other.

_____

_____

Has your deepened friendship with each other motivated you to be a 911 friend to others? If so, discuss together how God may be leading you to launch a "911 Friendship Strategy" within or outside your youth group.

_____

_____

Plan to discuss your "911 Friendship Strategy" with your youth group leader and group members when you next meet.

Special Request

Before completing your time together, would you help us? On the following page is the "Friendship 911 Evaluation Form." It would really help Josh McDowell and his ministry team if you would fill it out and send it to us. Thanks, and God bless you as you spread 911 friendship throughout your school and community!

Prayer

Close this time with your friendship partner in a prayer of thanks to God that He has chosen you to be His ambassador of friendship.

_____

_____

The PROJECT 911 Collection

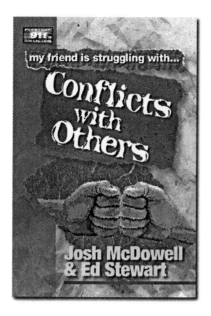

The story of Ken in this week's workbook is adapted from the small book entitled *My Friend Is Struggling with Conflicts with Others*. The book is designed as a giveaway book you can read and then give to a friend who wants to know how to resolve conflicts. Beyond the fictional story, this book provides practical steps to restoring friendship with parents and others.

If you need one or more of these books for you or a friend, contact your youth leader. He or she may have a number of copies on hand. If not, this and other books in this collection can be ordered in bulk by calling 1-800-933-9673 ext 9-2039. Or you may purchase copies of this book at your local Christian bookstore.

Friendship 911 Evaluation Form

How old are you?_____ ❑ Male ❑ Female

1. ❑ I went through this workbook with my youth group.

2. ❑ I went through this workbook by myself, not with my youth group.

3. How many of the Discovery Days did you complete?
❑ Very Few ❑ Some ❑ Most ❑ All

4. Did you meet with a friendship partner?
❑ Never ❑ A few times ❑ Very often ❑ Every week

5. Tell us how this workbook helped you the most.

_____

_____

_____

_____

6. Can you give us a suggestion on how to make these kinds of workbooks better?

_____

_____

_____

_____

_____

_____

_____

Please mail this form to:
Josh McDowell Ministry
P.O. Box 4126
Copley, OH 44321

Appendix

More about Intimate Life Ministries

Several times in this book I have mentioned the work of Dr. David Ferguson. This man's life and teaching have effected me profoundly over the past several years, so I want you to know something about him. David and his wife, Teresa, are the directors of Intimate Life Ministries.

What Is Intimate Life Ministries?

Intimate Life Ministries (ILM) is a training and resource ministry whose purpose is to *assist in the development of Great Commandment ministries worldwide.* Great Commandment ministries, designed to help us love God and our neighbors, are ongoing ministries that deepen our intimacy with God and with others in marriage, family, and the church.

Intimate Life Ministries comprises:

A network of **churches** seeking to fortify homes and communities with God's love

A network of **pastors and other ministry leaders** walking intimately with God and their families and seeking to live vulnerably before their people

A team of **accredited trainers** committed to helping churches establish ongoing Great Commandment ministries

A team of **professional associates** from ministry and other professional Christian backgrounds, assisting with research, training, and resource development

Christian broadcasters, publishers, media, and other affiliates, cooperating to see marriages and families reclaimed as divine relationships

Headquarters staff providing strategic planning, coordination, and support

How Can Intimate Life Ministries Serve You?

ILM's Intimate Life Network of Churches is an effective ongoing support and equipping relationship with churches and Christian leaders. There are at least four ways ILM can serve you:

Ministering to Ministry Leaders

ILM offers a unique two-day "Galatians 6:6" retreat to ministers and their spouses for personal renewal and for reestablishing and affirming ministry and family priorities. The conference accommodations and meals are provided as a gift to ministry leaders by cosponsoring partners. Thirty to forty such retreats are held throughout the U.S. and Europe each year.

Partnering with Denominations and Other Ministries

Numerous denominations and ministries have partnered with ILM by "commissioning" them to equip their ministry leaders through the Galatians 6:6 retreats along with strategic training and ongoing resources. This unique partnership enables a denomination to use the expertise of ILM trainers and resources to perpetuate a movement of Great Commandment ministry at the local level. ILM also provides a crisis-support setting in which denominations may send ministers, couples, or families who are struggling in their relationships.

Identifying, Training, and Equipping Lay Leaders

ILM is committed to helping the church equip its lay leaders through:

Sermon Series on several Great Commandment topics to help pastors communicate a vision for Great Commandment health as well as identify and cultivate a core lay leadership group.

Community Training Classes that provide weekly or weekend training to church staff and lay leaders. Classes are delivered by Intimate Life trainers along with ILM video-assisted training, workbooks, and study courses.

One-Day Training Conferences on implementing Great Commandment ministry in the local church through marriage, parenting, or singles ministry. Conducted by Intimate Life trainers, these conferences are a great way to jump-start Great Commandment ministry in a local church.

Providing Advanced Training and Crisis Support

ILM conducts advanced training for both ministry staff and lay leaders through the Leadership Institute, focusing on relational ministry (marriage, parenting, families, singles, men, women, blended families, and counseling). The Enrichment Center provides support to relationships in crisis through Intensive Retreats for couples, families, and singles.

For more information on how you, your church, or your denomination can take advantage of the many services and resources, such as the Great Commandment Ministry Training Resource offered by Intimate Life Ministries, write or call:

Intimate Life Ministries
P.O. Box 201808
Austin, TX 78720-1808
1-800-881-8008
www.ilmministries.org

CPSIA information can be obtained at www.ICGtesting.com
Printed in the USA
LVOW09s1112111013

356528LV00001B/2/A